Wit, Wisdom and Everything In Between

S RAMKUMAR

INDIA • SINGAPORE • MALAYSIA

Copyright © S Ramkumar 2024

All Rights Reserved.

ISBN

Paperback 979-8-89556-960-3

Hardcase 979-8-89588-692-2

This book has been published with all efforts taken to make the material error-free after the consent of the author. However, the author and the publisher do not assume and hereby disclaim any liability to any party for any loss, damage, or disruption caused by errors or omissions, whether such errors or omissions result from negligence, accident, or any other cause.

While every effort has been made to avoid any mistake or omission, this publication is being sold on the condition and understanding that neither the author nor the publishers or printers would be liable in any manner to any person by reason of any mistake or omission in this publication or for any action taken or omitted to be taken or advice rendered or accepted on the basis of this work. For any defect in printing or binding the publishers will be liable only to replace the defective copy by another copy of this work then available.

DEDICATION

To my beloved parents,

Your unwavering support, boundless love, and endless encouragement have been the bedrock of my journey all the way... Thank you for believing in me every step of the way.

To my wife, son, daughter in law and daughter,

"To my loving wife, the anchor of my soul and the light of my life. Your unwavering support and boundless love fill my days with warmth and joy. To my son, the embodiment of hope and promise, whose dreams inspire me endlessly. To my cherished daughter-in-law, a blessing to our family with her kindness, resilience, and unwavering dedication. To my daughter, a shining beacon of grace and strength, whose smile brightens even the darkest days and. May this book be a reminder of my endless gratitude for each of you and a tribute to the love that binds us together forever."

To my cherished readers,

This book is for you. Your curiosity, passion, and willingness to embark on this journey with me are the heartbeats of this book **"Wit, Wisdom and Everything In Between"** a sequel to **"Not just a joke book."** My first book **"Not Just a Joke Book"** has been very well received round the globe. May these pages make you smile, entertain, and resonate with you as deeply as they did with me.

With heartfelt gratitude,

S. Ramkumar

Contents

Acknowledgements

Mahatria Ra, globally celebrated as a spiritual leader and a beacon of spiritual living, has profoundly impacted millions, including myself. Over the past two decades, his wisdom and knowledge, coupled with his wit and humor, have greatly influenced me. His exceptional storytelling and the illustrative examples he shares about life and living are truly remarkable. I extend my heartfelt thanks to him.

Since the 20th century, stand-up comedy has evolved, finding new platforms in comedy clubs, campuses, television, and eventually the internet. My interactions with Bosskey, a prominent stand-up comedian in Chennai for about two decades, has profoundly influenced my perspective about people and viewpoints on a funny note. His multifaceted personality and funny comments on life at large has left a lasting impact on me, and I owe him my gratitude.

For over five decades, my cousin Chandrakant's unique perspectives, humorous logic, and storytelling abilities have been a great source of inspiration. I am deeply thankful to him.

Anoop Jaiswal, IPS, retired DGP of Tamil Nadu, has been my friend for more than a decade. His photographic memory allows him to recall events from 40 years ago with incredible precision. He exemplifies compassion, courage, wisdom, morals, and ethics. His storytelling skills are mesmerizing, and I have not encountered anyone who lives with such integrity. My big thanks to him.

Additionally, I have enjoyed YouTube videos by Thenkachi Swaminathan, Pulavar Shanmugha Vadivel, Pulavar Ramalingam, and Mohanasundaram. Although I do not know them personally, I am profoundly grateful for their wit and humor. They had indirectly influenced me to see the world in a lighter perspective.

Their ideas and perspectives, their narrative in person and through YouTube videos have helped me write this book. My heartfelt thanks to them.

S. Ramkumar

FOREWORD

It is my absolute pleasure to write the foreword for "Wit, Wisdom, and Everything in Between" by my dear friend, S Ramkumar. I've had the privilege of knowing Ramkumar for nearly four decades, and over the past 15 years, I've witnessed his remarkable transformation from a successful businessman to a dedicated philanthropist, social worker, spiritual seeker, and leadership developer.

In today's commercial world, it's rare to find someone who, at a relatively young age, relinquishes the pursuit of wealth and status to focus on serving others. Ramkumar's selfless journey is truly inspiring.

This book is a sequel to his well-received "Not Just a Joke Book," and I firmly believe it will surpass its predecessor. While it's filled with humor and wit, it also offers profound wisdom and philosophy gained through Ramkumar's extensive life experience.

Reading this book is reminiscent of classic Tamil comedy films – laughter and entertainment intertwined with valuable life lessons. I'd love to share examples, but I wouldn't want to spoil the thrill of discovery for readers.

Throughout these pages, Ramkumar subtly emphasizes the importance of living in the present, letting go of past regrets and future anxieties. He also stresses the significance of finding joy and wearing a smile, even in life's challenging moments.

I'm confident that this book won't be Ramkumar's last. His wealth of experience, coupled with his lifelong commitment to learning, ensures that he will continue to share his insights and inspire others.

I wholeheartedly commend "Wit, Wisdom, and Everything in Between" to anyone seeking a delightful and enriching experience.

S. PARAMASIVAN, MANAGING DIRECTOR, AFCONS INFRASTRUCTURE LTD, MUMBAI

ACKNOWLEDGEMENT TO MR S. PARAMASIVAN

I am deeply grateful to Mr. S. Paramasivan for his kindness and generosity in writing the foreword for my second book, *Wit, Wisdom, and Everything in Between*. His endorsement means the world to me.

Over the past four decades, I have had the privilege of witnessing Mr. Paramasivan's exceptional leadership and vision. His transformative efforts at Afcons Infrastructure Ltd. have propelled the company to remarkable heights, turning it into a towering success under his guidance.

What I find most inspiring, however, is the remarkable balance he maintains between his immense achievements and his humility. Like a kite soaring high, his accomplishments are truly awe-inspiring, yet his feet remain firmly grounded. His compassion, kindness, and commitment to society make him a role model for many.

Mr. S. Paramasivan has been a Whole-Time Director on the Board of Afcons Infrastructure Ltd. since 2002 and is currently serving as its Managing Director. With over 40 years of experience, he has played a pivotal role in the company's turnaround, consolidation, and growth, especially following its acquisition by the Shapoorji Pallonji Group.

An alumnus of the University of Madurai, Mr. Paramasivan holds a degree in Commerce. He is a Certified Associate of the Indian Institute of Bankers, a Fellow Member of The Institute of Cost Accountants of India, and The Institute of Company Secretaries of India. Additionally, he is a Stanford Certified Project Manager. His leadership extends beyond the company, as he actively contributes to the Taxation and Infrastructure Committees of CII, serves as Co-Chair of the Infrastructure Committee of FICCI, and plays a vital role in various Indo-African initiatives.

Thank you, Mr. Paramasivan, for your invaluable support and the inspiration you continue to provide through your exemplary life and career...and for writing the Foreword of the book, "Wit, Wisdom and Everything in Between.

S. Ramkumar

1. Graffiti

Patient: Doctor, the medicine you wrote on the top left of my prescription isn't available in any pharmacy in Mumbai.

Doctor: That's not medicine. I was just checking if my pen was working, doodling.

Patient: What! Because of your terrible handwriting, I had to visit fifty-two shops trying to find it.

One pharmacist told me he'd get it for me tomorrow.

Another said the company is closed and offered a similar medicine from a different company.

A third mentioned it's in high demand and only available on the black market.

The fourth one scared me, saying it's a cancer medication and asked if someone at my place has cancer.

2. Salary Hike

Employee: Excuse me, sir. May I talk to you for a moment?

Boss: Sure, come on in. What can I do for you?

Employee: Well, sir, as you know, I've been with this prestigious firm for over ten years.

Boss: Yes, I'm aware.

Employee: I'll get straight to the point. I'd like to request a raise. I currently have four companies pursuing me, so I wanted to discuss it with you first.

Boss: A raise? I'd love to give you one, but this just isn't the right time.

Employee: I understand and I know the current economic downturn has impacted sales. However, please consider my hard work, proactiveness, and loyalty to this company for over a decade.

Boss: Considering those factors, and because I don't want to risk losing valuable talent, I'm willing to offer you a ten percent raise and an extra five days of vacation time. How does that sound?

Employee: That sounds great! It's a deal. Thank you, sir!

Boss: Before you go, just out of curiosity, which companies were after you?

Employee: Oh, the Electric Company, Gas Company, Water Company, and the Mortgage Company!

3. Today's Mood

Q: Hello, what's up today?

A: My stress levels!

4. Well-settled in Life

When searching for a prospective bridegroom, people typically post advertisements on matrimonial sites that look like this:

"Seeking a well-settled man aged 27-30, taller than 5'8", belonging to this religion, caste, and creed. The prospective groom should be a postgraduate, preferably with an engineering background and an MBA. Preferred locations are the US, UK, Southeast Asia, and UAE."

The process usually follows three steps:

1. Age, weight, height, sex.

2. Caste, creed, religion.

3. Job, qualifications, place of work.

Rarely do these ads mention qualities more relevant to marriage, such as upbringing, affection, love, family attachment, kindness, honesty, humility, and virtues.

It seems that all people want is someone who is well-settled.

One man saw a classified advertisement in the local newspaper and thought he was eligible to propose, especially since he met the "well-settled" requirement along with the other criteria. Unfortunately, while he was well-settled, he was already married!

5. Beware of Dogs

An English teacher went to visit his friend at his house. As he was about to open the main gate, he noticed a sign that read, "Beware of dogs." Peering inside, he was surprised to see only one dog tied to a leash. "According to grammar, there should be more than one dog," he thought to himself. Confident he could manage the single dog, he boldly opened the gate.

Awoken by the noise, the watchman sprang up and began shouting at the intruder, "Who are you? What do you want? Why did you open the gate? Whom do you want to meet?" Meanwhile, the dog remained a silent witness to the watchman's tirade.

At that moment, the teacher understood the truth behind the sign. The owner had been accurate: one dog was tied up, but the other was not.

6. Anticipate Challenges

A schoolboy sent a veiled text message to his mother from school: "Mom, failed in science and maths. Please prepare dad."

His mother replied, "Dad is well-prepared. You should come prepared too."

7. Poor Host, Rich Lesson

Mrs Sudha Murthy, the wife of Mr Narayana Murthy, Co-Founder of Infosys, shares an incident from many decades ago that offers food for thought.

A bit of background on Mrs. Sudha Murthy: she is an engineer specialising in electrical and electronic engineering. Her father was a surgeon, and her mother was a school teacher. She has received the Padma Shri and Padma Bhushan awards for her contributions to education and social welfare. On March 8, 2024, she became a Member of Parliament in the Rajya Sabha.

Shortly after their wedding, Mr. and Mrs. Narayana Murthy were invited to dinner at a very rich man's home. After exchanging pleasantries and enjoying a sumptuous meal provided by the host, it was time for the Murthys to leave. The host also presented them with a wonderful gift.

On their way back, Mrs. Sudha Murthy remarked to her husband, "I have never met a poorer man in my life!" Surprised, Mr. Murthy asked what made her think so.

Mrs. Sudha Murthy explained, "They are so poor that they could not even afford a few books to display in their drawing room." "No matter how rich you are, if you don't have books in the drawing room, you are extremely poor!"

8. Irreversible Act

One evening, an office assistant was working late at the government hcadquarters.

Around 9 p.m., as he stepped out of his office, he noticed the Cabinet Minister standing by the classified document shredder in the hallway, holding a piece of paper.

"Do you know how to work this thing?" the Cabinet Minister asked. "My executive assistant has gone home, and I don't know how to use it."

"Yes, sir," the office assistant replied. He turned on the machine, took the paper from the Cabinet Minister, and fed it into the shredder.

"Now," said the Cabinet Minister, "I just need one copy..."

9. Sleep is Vital for Everyone

At night, he heard the sound of a dog outside the house and came out to notice the high pedigree dog standing in front of the gate of his house.

It seemed to stand still for a long time. It was staring at him. He was a bit surprised.

Even after a few minutes, it was still staring at him.

He whistled softly. Immediately, it ran in on all fours and stood by him. He caressed its neck. In return, it licked his feet.

Then I went to the corner of the room, lay down on a rug, and was fast asleep in a minute.

The man is now confused. Whose dog was it? Some rich man's dog, he thought.

Its appearance, buckled belt, muscular body, he understood that it was well-bred and nourished.

The dog, however, came here for what? He was very confused.

After going to bed at night, he wakes up in the morning, takes a bath, changes his clothes, finishes his breakfast, and leaves for the office. He told the servant and left. In the evening, the dog was not there. On enquiry, the servant said that she had left in the afternoon.

The next night. Same time again. Same dog. Similarly, she came inside and cuddled with him for a while and fell asleep in the same place. In the evening, the dog was not there.

This incident continued for several days.

Where did the dog come from after leaving the house? He could not find it.

One day, he wrote the details on a piece of paper and tied it around his neck.

When the dog came back the next day, it had another piece of paper around its neck.

The man read it, and after reading it, he was rolling around in laughter. The worker didn't understand anything and asked, "What was written like that to make you laugh so much?"

The message said, "Greetings to you, sir." This dog is mine.

"It was because of my wife's snoring in the night that made the dog leave home, I guess." It had been disappearing at night for a few days. Through their letter, I came to know that it is sleeping peacefully in your house.

"Thank you so much for your love."

P.S. "One request. Can I come with the dog from tomorrow?"

It's been months since I've slept well...

10. Updates About Family Affairs

Dear son,

I am well, and I do hope that you are also doing well.

Extremely happy to inform you that dad has finally got a job. He now has 1000 people working under him. He has been assigned the prestigious job of cutting grass at the cemetery.

The weather here isn't so bad. It rained only twice last week. The first time it rained for 3 days, and the second time it rained for 4 days.

I was going to send you some cash, but before I realised, I had sealed the envelope.

Since nothing much has happened, there's nothing more to add.

Love, Mom.

11. Bottom Up

This is a beautifully constructed message. First, read from top to bottom, then from bottom to top. See the difference.

Leader: Yes, now the right time has come.

Public: Will you loot the nation?

Leader: Oh, no.

Public: Will you work for us?

Leader: Yes, very much.

Public: Will you increase the prices and cost of living?

Leader: Don't think about that.

Public: Will you provide us jobs and livelihood?

Leader: Surely, I will do that.

Public: Will you do scams and misappropriations.

Leader: Are you mad? Absolutely not.

Public: Can we believe in and trust you?

Leader: Yes.

Public: Oh, our leader.

The leader won the election and was re-elected. Now read from bottom to top.

12. Restless Monkey Mind Syndrome

A restless monkey is a happy monkey. We all have a restless monkey mind swinging between our ears. Even on a holiday meant to relax us, our minds wander. We struggle to be present and appreciate the wonders of nature. Standing before a majestic, snow-clad mountain, we try to capture the moment, but it slips away almost instantly as we fidget with our phones.

We're so accustomed to noise and constant activity that our lives lack those "AHA!" moments, leaving us with mere "Oh!" reactions. Even when witnessing the Taj Mahal or Niagara Falls for the first time, there's little excitement. People immediately reach for their phones to take pictures. If we can't savour the moment, what's the point of capturing it? As the saying goes, "When the 'live' experience itself isn't absorbing, what can a recorded version convey?" Thus, landmarks like the Taj Mahal and Niagara Falls become just another casual thing.

Consider the story of a businessman from Mumbai. Used to the constant noise of his house on the main road, he found the silence of his relatives' village unbearable. Unable to sleep in the quiet, he called his office in Mumbai and asked them to record the noise of the main road. Once he received the recording, he played it and slept peacefully like a baby.

13. Proving Right or Winning

You know that you are a mature person when you can be right without proving the other person wrong. This way you can avoid inner conflict because you realise in the end that inner peace is far more important than proving that you are right. However, people get lured by their ego to prove themselves right at any cost to satiate their egos, forgetting their primary objective of moving on to get their things done and getting ahead is forgotten! Haven't we heard of the phrase "Winning the battle but losing the war!" Battles are usually short-term and wars are long-term. Here, battle is a metaphor for proving ourselves right and satisfying the ego, and war is a metaphor for achieving our primary objective and moving on. However, we have to be doing the right things and not slacken.

The importance of remembering bedtime stories that parents tell their children cannot be more pertinent if we start implementing them in our lives. One of the stories goes like this – Once there was a village that had a river in between. The villagers built a narrow bridge to cross it. One day, one goat was crossing the bridge and halfway it faced another goat approaching from the other side. There wasn't much space for the two of them to cross one another. Both goats waited for the other to turn back, but none of them relented. One goat said, "I am older than you, so let me pass first." The other goat said, "But I came first," and the arguments led to a bitter fight since none of them wanted to compromise their positions. Soon their arguments turned into blows, and one goat struck the other with its horns; the other goat retaliated. The fight was intense, and soon both goats lost their balance; they fell into the river and were washed away by the currents.

After some time, two more goats met in the middle of the bridge coming from the opposite direction. This time, one of the goats thought for a while and said, "The bridge is narrow and both of us cannot cross at the same time, so I will lie down and you carefully walk over me." The other goat realised that this was the most sensible thing to do. He appreciated the other goat's wisdom. The wise goat lay on the bridge, and the other goat walked over him, and both of them reached the other sides. They were across each other and they were across the bridge!! What mattered more was crossing the bridge and not who crossed first. The moral of the story is that anger and ego lead to destruction while humility leads to fulfilment.

Akhilesh was a VP - Sales in a corporate company. In the first quarter of the business calendar, he had not met the sales target on all the five verticals he was looking after – Banking, Insurance, Healthcare, Manufacturing, and education since business was sluggish. He was quite confident that he would catch up in the next quarter and perhaps even exceed the target should he receive a sizeable marketing budget. After all, it was a global recession and it applied to all businesses uniformly. He had not slackened but the general mood was not favouring sales. He was certain that with a little marketing and advertising campaign, he would certainly perform well in the next quarter.

In the review meeting to discuss the status of the business, all the heads of departments were present – Marketing, Finance, Operations, HR, and IT. It was Akhilesh's turn. He had made power points with graphs, Excel sheets with numbers, and was thorough with the figures within his area of work. The meeting was going well when suddenly the CFO said, "Mr. Akhilesh, somehow, I get the feeling that you have not done your work well in the manufacturing division."

Akhilesh was not quite prepared for this comment. He rebuked, saying, "With so many setbacks in the manufacturing division, which by itself is a tough department to handle, it gets compounded due to the fact that payments are delayed because the finance department had delayed payments due to the party." He further added, saying, "You are immensely wrong, Mr. CFO. You guys sit in flower-bedded seats on the top floor with no clue as to what is taking place in the real world. You should limit the distance and move to the floor below." The CFO was offended and expressed sharp disapproval of the way Akhilesh was handling things, as Akhilesh's rebuke set his head spinning.

The Chairman adjourned the meeting with a coffee break to break the impasse. However, the mood was not different after the coffee break, and the standoff between the two was palpable. The "Joie de vivre" was lost as well as the focus and discussed strategies to move. So much is the power of negative emotions that strangulates the very joy of life. At the beginning of the meeting, everyone was with Akhilesh, but after his backlash and faceoff with the CFO, everyone started agreeing with the CFO's point of view. Akhilesh's marketing budget was further reduced at the end of the meeting. There were even talks that he would get transferred.

If we consider why things went haywire, the reason is the response of the VP – Marketing to a cursory comment by the CFO that the manufacturing division had not done well. However, the CFO had indirectly conveyed that the other departments had done well. Akhilesh had four options in front of him as a response to his assumed transgression by the CFO. 1. He could have agreed straightaway since that was a fact. 2. He could have disagreed politely. 3. He could have asked the CFO, "Sir, can you kindly help organise this?" 4. He could have smilingly moved to the next point in the agenda without disagreeing. Reacting and wanting to prove that he was right and not able to deal with the stressful situation proved to be the breaking point for Akhilesh who was considering tendering a resignation letter even as the best way out.

As in the goat's story, when you are crossing a narrow bridge with an opponent on the other side, it helps to retrace your steps back and allow your opponent to cross, leaving him bemused, and you cross subsequently! The sure, certain way to invalidate people who confront you is to agree with them. This really shakes them and leaves them distracted. Crossing the bridge is important; it does not matter who crosses first! It's not a race. It's a point of view. It's a perspective. It's an attitude. However, we should always prove to ourselves that we are doing the right thing and keep moving towards our goal.

14. The Role of Thieves in Our Economy

The teacher instructed the children to write an essay on thieves for the next day.

A Class XII student wrote the following essay:

"Thieves are the backbone of the country's economy."

This statement might sound like a joke or seem incorrect, but it is a subject worth considering.

Security Products Industry: Safes, cupboards, and locks are necessary because of thieves, providing jobs for the companies that manufacture these items.

Home Security: Thieves necessitate the installation of window grills, doors, locks, and additional security measures. This creates employment for many people in related industries.

Residential and Commercial Security: Due to thieves, compounds are built around houses, shops, and societies. There are gates, guards stationed 24 hours a day, and uniforms for these guards, all contributing to employment.

Security Technology: Thieves drive the demand for CCTV cameras, metal detectors, and cyber cells.

Law Enforcement: Thieves ensure the existence of police forces, police stations, patrol cars, batons, rifles, revolvers and bullets, all of which provide jobs.

Judicial System: The presence of thieves necessitates courts, judges, lawyers, clerks, and bail bondsmen, creating employment within the judicial system.

Penal System: Thieves require the existence of jails, jailers, and police officers for the jails, further creating jobs.

Consumer Economy: When items like mobile phones, laptops, electronic devices, bicycles, and vehicles are stolen, people buy new ones, which boosts the economy and provides work for many.

Media Coverage: If a thief becomes highly recognised and famous, both domestic and international media gain content, supporting their livelihood.

After considering all this, one might be convinced that thieves are indeed an integral part of the entire governmental system and a source of livelihood for many people in society.

15. Disparity in Compensation: When Changing Valves

At a car mechanic workshop, the chief mechanic, who also owned the workshop, was removing the cylinder, piston, and valves of a Mercedes Benz GLS model. He noticed a renowned cardiologist waiting for the service manager to report on his car, which had been experiencing some issues.

The mechanic set down his tools and approached the cardiologist. "It's ironic," he said, "that both of us do similar work, but the compensation is vastly different. You earn ten times more for changing a valve, while I do the same for much less. It's unfair."

The cardiologist cleared his throat and replied, "Try changing the valve while the engine is running!"

16. Before You Fire an Employee

I received a call from my site supervisor when they were marking the plan of the approved drawing on the floor to simulate the feeling of how the floor arrangements would look like before commencing the interior work. The clients were also there along with my interior designer who had made the design. The design was done after a few rounds of discussions and changing the design a few times. A reception, a meeting room, seventy-five workstations, a room for the CEO, a conference room, 5 VPs, a pantry, toilets, and an electrical room. Finally, the design looked perfect and then the marking began, and after the marking, the call came...

The design on the paper and the actual plan in the office while doing the marking on the floor were not accordant. The measurements taken by the designer initially were wrong by miles, so the plan went awfully wrong. The clients were furious, and I had to cut a sorry figure. However, we took the measurements again with another designer from our office since the clients had lost their trust in the initial designer. Working extra time, we were able to complete the drawing the next day and marked the plan on the floor. The design on the paper matched the plan on the floor. The clients' faith in us was restored.

That was not the first instance where my designer had made a mistake. He had committed a mistake in the plan when he had made the height of the table as 1'6" instead of 2'6". I thought about the designer's performance. My immediate repercussion was to fire the designer for his carelessness which affected our work. I also thought about his earlier works. He had performed extremely well, and his designs were spot on with not a sq.ft of wastage. The last 4 months he was not in his elements. I had a habit of documenting all our personnel's performances, and so when I made a tabulation of all the good designs my designer had made and placed it along with the list of designs that were not made so well, I could see a stark difference between the two. The number of good designs was far more than the recent careless ones. I made up my mind not to fire him but to have a chat with him.

I called my designer and after some time went on to tell him that his earlier designs were so commendable in the past, but how was it that suddenly the designs were all wrong? Taking measurements was wrong, communication with the supervisor was wrong; everything about his performance was wrong.

My designer broke down then and said that because of the poor health of his young son, all the mistakes were happening. He said that his son had blood cancer. I broke down then. How unfairly one could judge a person from the outside. What do we know about what the other person is going through? We are so judgemental and immediately come to conclusions and make wrong decisions. Luckily for me, I would have fired my designer but for the documentation I had, which showed many pluses and very few minuses.

My designer was a shy person and was keeping it all to himself. Had he opened up even in the earlier stages, things would have been a lot different. We would have given him that emotional support as well. I told him to take time off after handing over the work in hand to another designer and join once the time was appropriate.

After 2 weeks, I received a call from my designer saying that his son had passed away. I attended the funeral and told him to take more time off. He said that he would join the following Monday, and sure enough, he did. He was as efficient and creative in his designs as he used to be before.

17. Call from the Income Tax Department

In 2010, I closed my business to dedicate myself to social service at the Ramakrishna Mutt and the Theosophical Society in Chennai. Naturally, I had to go through the systematic procedures of audits for income tax, service tax, and sales tax, given that I had run the company for a long time. It took me about 3-4 years to finally wrap everything up.

After announcing the closure, most employees left, so I ended up handling most tasks myself, including answering calls, following up on old payments, and paying creditors.

One day, around 2012, I was deeply engrossed in my accounts when I received a phone call. Casually, I picked up and said, "Hello." The person on the other end authoritatively stated, "We are calling on behalf of your sales tax, service tax, and income tax."

Hearing that it was regarding my taxes, I immediately sat up straight and responded, "Yes, sir, please tell me." The voice on the other end suddenly softened and said, "Sir, we handle the filing of sales tax, income tax, and service tax. Do you have any requirements, sir?"

I was furious and shouted at the person. Before I could express my frustration about the nuisance caused by such calls, he hung up. No one likes spam or marketing calls as they disrupt our peace.

Thankfully, the Truecaller app has been a great boon since then, helping to avoid many such telemarketers and spam calls.

My friend Bosskey, a stand-up comedian, has a way of dealing with telemarketers. If there is a call from, let's say, "Axis Bank,"

Telemarketer: Sir, I am calling from Axis Bank.

Bosskey: Yes, tell me, I am the MD of Axis Bank.

Line goes dead!

18. Lessons from Charlie Chaplin

Charlie Chaplin, one of the greatest humourists of all time, was an English comic actor and filmmaker whose career spanned about 75 years. During a public appearance on stage in a European country, he told a joke that received a standing ovation, as it was the custom of that country to stand and applaud whenever someone said something spectacular.

After the crowd settled down, Chaplin told the same joke again. This time, the audience looked at each other, and only those in the front row stood up and clapped. When he told the joke for the third time, there was pin-drop silence, and no one stood up.

Chaplin then remarked, "If even a good joke that makes you happy can only make you laugh once or twice, I wonder why people can remember all the unhappy things that happened long ago in life. People can insult you, but the person who insulted you will remember it only for a minute, forget and move on. However, those who were insulted remember it for ages and seek revenge to balance things."

Charlie Chaplin emphasised that it is wrong to hold on to any negative emotions.

Yesterday was over yesterday.

19. People Don't Forget the Way You Made Them Feel

At the "Maximum" city of Mumbai, a well-known psychiatrist met a young woman in his clinic. She had a problem. She was not getting along well with her boss. She liked her salary and the job but could not get along well with the boss. She tried her best to do a good job but somehow the boss was displeased with her work. It was not a one-off occasion but kept happening all the time.

She contemplated committing suicide, and before committing that draconian crime, she had the maturity to consult a psychiatrist, and that was the reason why she was there. The psychiatrist thought about it for a while and asked a few questions regarding her office, her job, her position, and her manager.

He took some time to try to mitigate her suffering by offering a solution that could work. The psychiatrist said, "It's easy to commit suicide; only cowards do that act. You aren't a coward." Just do what I suggest: "Please remember that no one is all good in counts and no one is all bad in all measures." From what I understand, he is not a bad guy. I am certainly sure that he has some good qualities in him." "Please mention to him sincerely the good qualities that he has." "Come and see me after a month," the psychiatrist said.

A month passed, and the lady did not turn up. The psychiatrist was worried if she had committed something stupid. After two months, the woman showed up, and her smile lit up the room. "Tell me what happened?" "Did things work out for you?"

The woman beamed at him and said that not only did things work out for me, I am happy to invite you to my wedding. Saying this, she handed over the invitation card.

The psychiatrist was very happy at the turn of events and asked her, "Who is the lucky man?" "Who else, but my manager only!"

20. Wisdom, Understanding, and Judgement

One of my relatives from abroad came home many years ago. He asked me if he could see a lawyer who is a specialist in the real estate segment. My relative wanted to find out whether he could invest in a piece of real estate in Chennai. He had all the necessary documents that a lawyer would call for before advising his client about his opinion on proceeding with an investment in real estate or not.

I knew a person who was good in the legal profession and after appraising my relative took him to meet the lawyer. The lawyer asked my relative a few questions, scrutinised the parent documents, agreement copies and told my relative, "You can go ahead and buy the property."

My relative was thrilled. He asked, "How much are the fees?" The lawyer replied, "Rs 5,000." My relative was a different person now when he heard the fees, especially after he got to know that the papers were alright. He asked the lawyer, "Why so much for the fees? You just skimmed through the pages and are charging me so much. Can you provide any justification and a breakdown of costs?"

The lawyer, an old man, had a naughty smile on his lips and displayed the split-up of costs:

Scrutinising all the papers: Rs 500

Understanding, wisdom, judging, and advising you to go ahead with the purchase: Rs 4500. (Wisdom and understanding come from years of experience and practice – judgement follows...)

Effort can never supersede wisdom, understanding, and judgement.

21. Effort and Expertise

A giant ship's engine broke down, and the ship's owners brought in several 'professionals' to fix it, but none could solve the problem.

Then they called an old man who had been repairing ships since he was young. He arrived with a large bag of tools and immediately began to work. He inspected the engine thoroughly from top to bottom.

Two of the ship's owners watched anxiously, hoping he could fix it. After a careful examination, the old man took a small hammer from his bag and gently tapped a specific spot. Instantly, the engine roared back to life. He put his hammer away, and the engine was fixed!

A week later, the owners received a Rs. 1,00,000 invoice from the old man.

"What?!" the owners exclaimed. "This old man hardly did anything!"

So, they wrote to the man, asking for an itemised invoice.

The man sent back an invoice that read:

- Tapping with a hammer: Rs. 1,000

- Knowing where to tap: Rs. 99,900

Effort is important, but experience and expertise, coupled with the intellect in knowing where to direct that effort, make all the difference.

22. Paradox of Life

52

Education took us from thumb impression to signature.

Technology took us from signature to thumb impression.

23. Mastering Happiness – The Watermelon Lesson

This document contains information about a YouTube video titled "Mastering Happiness: The Watermelon Lesson" that aims to inspire viewers on their life journey. The video uses a short story to deliver a motivational message emphasising the importance of following one's heart, embracing happiness, and persevering through challenges.

Once upon a time in a small village, there lived a wise old monk. He was known far and wide for his wisdom and sense of humour. One day, a young and eager student named Sam approached the master and said, "Master, I want to learn the secret to happiness and success. Please teach me."

Master Sito looked at Sam with a twinkle in his eye and said, "Very well, young one. But first, you must complete a simple task. Go to the market and buy the biggest, juiciest watermelon you can find. Then carry it on your head and walk through the village without dropping it."

Sam was puzzled but determined. He went to the market and found a massive watermelon. Balancing it on his head, he walked through the village with utmost concentration. As he passed by, people couldn't help but laugh and cheer him on. Some even joined in, clapping and making funny faces.

Finally, after a bumpy journey, Sam reached Master Sito's hut. The watermelon was intact, and Sam was relieved. He looked at Master Sito, expecting to be praised for his accomplishment.

But Master Sito burst into laughter. "Well done, young one," he exclaimed, wiping tears of mirth from his eyes. "You see, the secret to happiness and success is simple. Just like carrying that watermelon, life can be full of challenges and unexpected twists. But if you face them with a 'light heart and a sense of humour,' you will find joy even in the toughest moments."

Sam couldn't help but laugh too, realising the wisdom in Master Sito's words. From that day on, he approached life with a smile, facing challenges with the same determination he used to carry that watermelon. Whenever he felt overwhelmed, he would remember the funny watermelon lesson and find the strength to keep going.

You see, in life, embrace challenges with a sense of humour, and you will find that life's journey becomes a joyful adventure filled with laughter and success. Stay determined, but don't take yourself too seriously. Whenever you feel down or defeated, remember something funny that once happened to you.

24. Read and Reflect – You Might Find One Amongst You!

Once, there was a washerman who owned a donkey and a dog. One night, while the world slept, a thief broke into the house. The washerman was fast asleep, but the donkey and the dog were awake. The dog, feeling neglected and wanting to teach the master a lesson, decided not to bark.

The donkey, worried, said to the dog that if he didn't bark, the donkey would have to act. The dog remained stubborn, and the donkey began to bray loudly.

Hearing the donkey bray, the thief ran away. The master woke up and, thinking the donkey was braying for no reason, began to beat him.

Moral of the story: "One must not engage in duties other than their own."

Now, consider the same story from a different perspective...

The washerman was an educated man from a premier management institute. He had the talent to see the bigger picture and think outside the box. He was convinced there must be a reason for the donkey's braying. He stepped outside, did some fact-finding, and applied a bottom-up approach. He discovered that a thief had broken in and the donkey was trying to alert him. Impressed by the donkey's initiative and going beyond the call of duty, he rewarded him with plenty of hay and other perks, making him the master's favourite pet.

The dog's life didn't change much, except now the donkey was more motivated to do the dog's duties as well. During the annual appraisal, the dog managed to get a "ME" (Met Expectations).

Soon, the dog realised that the donkey was taking care of his duties, allowing him to enjoy a life of sleeping and lazing around.

The donkey was rated as a "star performer," but soon became overburdened with work, always under pressure, and began looking for a new job.

25. Why Our Clothes No Longer Fit?

Bio dialogue: It Actually Happens!

Unless you've just run a marathon or climbed Mount Everest, your body can't handle the junk food we consume—like samosas, bread pakoras, and doughnuts from the hospital canteen. Most of these foods are packed with sugar, fats, and refined starch.

When this flood of glucose hits the bloodstream, alarms go off in the liver and pancreas. At the genome level (total DNA in a cell), a metabolic "switchboard" lights up. The bio dialogue goes like this:

Liver to Pancreas: Glucose levels are skyrocketing! What's your plan?

Pancreas: I'm exhausted from handling the aloo paratha from breakfast. And that super sweet milky masala chai and egg at 9:00. You've got to take this load.

Liver: I've got no room. Hits panic button. Sirens going off.

Genome: Come on, liver, convert the glucose to glycogen.

Liver: I'm bursting with glycogen. Let me call the muscles. See if they need any energy.

Muscles: What? Energy? No, we have no need for energy. We haven't moved much in weeks.

Genome: Well, liver, what's your plan?

Liver: I'll convert the glucose to triglycerides and store it in the bloodstream.

Bloodstream: No way! Blood is already so thick; circulation through capillary beds is at critical levels. We've got billions of starving and suffocating cells in the toes, eyes, brain, and kidneys.

Genome: That can only mean one thing. Liver, you know what to do.

Liver: Okay! It'll take a few hours, but I can send these triglycerides to adipose tissue. Let me see... belly, butt, thighs... back of the arms, a little under the chin. That'll have to do.

And that's how our clothes no longer fit!

When we see such food, it starts with an argument between the tongue and brain. The brain says, "Don't touch it, you already have enough of it in your system. Instead, have fresh fruits and vegetables." The tongue replies, "I cannot resist the temptation. Please be quiet."

Need to remember that health is in our hands.

26. Yoga Day Success

The guy in the medical shop was very happy, laughing loudly, and feeling proud of himself.

A customer who went into the shop asked the medical shop owner, "Why are you so happy?"

The medical shop owner said, "Yesterday was yoga day... By evening yesterday, all my Iodex, Tiger Balm, Moov, Reli spray... all those got sold out. Knowingly I had stocked many!"

27. A Tale of Reliability and Accountability

Once upon a time, there lived an old and pious man, renowned for his honesty. One day, his neighbour, a wealthy merchant, came to him with a request. The merchant was about to embark on a voyage and asked the old man to safeguard his wealth until his return. The old man agreed and, with God as his witness, promised to protect and safeguard the merchant's wealth.

The old man then entrusted the safekeeping of the merchant's wealth to his son, making him swear an oath of propriety and honesty. However, the son began to dip into the merchant's wealth. People noticed this and warned the old man of his son's misdeeds. When confronted, the son dismissed the accusations as rumours and idle gossip from jealous people who couldn't bear to see his prosperity. The old man accepted his son's explanation, and things continued as before.

When the merchant returned, he demanded his wealth back. The old man called his son, who handed over only a quarter of the merchant's wealth, claiming that was all there was. Realising he had been cheated, the merchant approached the king. The king listened to the merchant's complaint and summoned the old man. The old man came to court with his son and, handing him over to the king, said, "Your Majesty, the merchant is right. My son has confessed to the crime. Please punish him."

The king had the son flogged and imprisoned. He then praised the old man's honesty and dismissed the case. However, the merchant demanded punishment for the old man, saying, "I have still not received justice. I entrusted my wealth to the old man, who swore by God to safeguard it. While the old man's integrity remains intact, I have been robbed of my life's savings and made a pauper. It was the old man's decision to entrust my wealth to his son for safekeeping. As far as I am concerned, the old man is the culprit and should be punished."

Though the old man was neither a party to the theft nor benefited from it, and he had even sent his son to jail, the merchant insisted on the old man's punishment. The Betal then asked Vikramaditya, "What should the king's decision be?"

Vikramaditya replied, "Though the old man is innocent of the actual theft, he is guilty of dereliction of duty. The son's crime was straightforward, but the old man's was graver. He did nothing to protect the merchant's wealth. Far from being vigilant, he failed to take action even when warned of his son's misdeeds. Because of his laxity, the merchant is condemned to a life of penury. The old man should be punished."

The world is suffering not because of the violence of bad people but because of the silence of good people. Accountability is described as the responsibility of not only what we do but also what we were supposed to do but did not do.

28. Fundamental Needs of a Traveller

A traveller went into a hotel reception and asked, "Can you give me a room and a bath, please?"

The man at the counter said, "Of course, I can give you a room, but you have to take your own bath, please!"

29. Welcome Drink

In the early nineties, there was an airline in India called East West Airlines. Many of us believe in the saying, "First impressions are the best impressions." To welcome travellers and make them feel comfortable on board, the flight attendants were instructed to serve welcome drinks, but only soft drinks! Shortly after the passengers were seated, the flight attendants would come around with the drinks.

Passengers appreciated this thoughtful gesture and were enthusiastic about the idea. However, there was one amusing incident. After enjoying his welcome drink, a passenger pressed the call button above his seat. When the flight attendant arrived and asked what he needed, the passenger replied, "Can you welcome me again?"

The passenger who sat next to him, and soon everyone wanted the attendants to welcome them all again. No more were they welcomed!

30. It's Just Not in Your Name

Five students—Dinesh, Saransh, Joshua, Abraham, and Nizar—were walking through the college campus toward the cafeteria. From about 50 feet behind, the professor of the psychology department, who was also walking toward the cafeteria, called out, "Hey, Dinesh." Dinesh turned, greeted the professor, and continued walking.

Next, the professor called Saransh, who turned back, said, "Good morning, sir," and kept walking. When the professor called Joshua, Joshua warmly turned back and wished the professor.

Despite these exchanges, the students and the professor maintained the same 50-foot distance. The professor then called Abraham, who turned back, conveyed his wishes, and continued walking. When the professor called out to Nizar, Nizar also turned back and warmly greeted him.

As they approached the cafeteria, the professor suddenly shouted, "Idiot!" All five students turned back, completely puzzled.

31. A Complaint Too Far

The inspector in the police station was sipping his coffee in the afternoon. A luxury car came by, and as the driver parked the car near the police station, a young woman stepped out of the car. With an air of pride, she walked past the reception and went straight to the inspector.

Without greeting him, she sat down on the chair in front of the inspector. She said, "I have come here to lodge a complaint against my tailor."

Inspector: What is the complaint, madam?

Woman: This blessed tailor of mine is not picking up my call. I don't have his address. I want to pull him by the ear and give him a mouthful.

Inspector: Did you give him your clothes?

Woman: No

Inspector: Did you give him any money?

Woman: No

Inspector: Did he misbehave with you?

Woman: No, he was indeed very polite and nice.

Inspector: You have come here to lodge a complaint. Unless there is some malice, some cheating, I can't take up the case. Tell me in what way the tailor has cheated you?

Woman: He ran away with my measurements!

Inspector: Please give the tailor's number; I will tell him to return it!

Imagine the plight of policing!

32. What is the Work of God?

Many years back, there was a haughty king who ruled a kingdom, and the subjects were fearing his wrath caused by his excessive pride. One day, the king called his learned minister and asked him, "What is the work of God?" The minister thought for a while and told him, "Your Majesty, the work of God is to create." The king was not pleased with his answer; he said, "By tomorrow, if you do not give a satisfactory reply, your head will be severed." The minister rued over the situation and was passing by a field in contemplation to get the answer.

A farmer came from the paddy field where he was working and asked the minister, "Sir, what are you worrying about?" The minister told his predicament. The farmer thought for a while and said, "Please take me to the king and I will clear his doubts for sure." The next day the farmer was introduced to the king in his court. The king asked the farmer, "Do you have the answer? If so, tell me now." The farmer bowed before the king and said, "Your Majesty, can you come down from the throne, all of the eleven steps and I will tell you the answer." The king thought for a while and came down the eleven steps and was alongside the farmer and the minister. The farmer quickly climbed the eleven steps and sat on the throne. The king got confused. He roared to the farmer who was occupying his position and asked him, "What on earth are you doing?" The farmer said, "Your Majesty, what was your question, can you ask it again?" The king was extremely angry but asked the same question he asked the minister, "What is God's work after he created the world?" The farmer had a twinkle in his eye and explained to the king, "As much as God creates and brings the best in people, he also dislikes pride and vanity and brings down people who act so.

"God can bring down anyone in a matter of seconds. This is just an example, and if you mend your ways, there will be cooperation and harmony in our kingdom," he said. "Pride cometh before the fall." The king understood his folly, became a changed man, and ruled his empire well. The king was lucky to have good advice. We might not be so lucky if we are not careful.

The strength of pride must eventually surrender to the power of humility. In the whole of our short stay on this planet, let us all refrain from letting pride come in our way. Pride is spiritual cancer. It eats up the very possibility of love, contentment, or common sense. Stay humble and accountable in your walk with the Lord.

33. Alimony

In a family court, the judge listened to both the husband and wife who sought a divorce after ten years of marriage. The judge made earnest efforts to persuade the couple to stay together, perhaps suggesting a temporary separation. However, both the husband and wife were adamant, especially the husband.

The judge warned the husband that he would have to pay 50% of his income as alimony to his wife each month. This prompted the husband to burst into uncontrollable laughter. Annoyed, the judge asked why he found the situation amusing in such a serious setting that would determine his future.

"My Lord," said the husband, "I've been giving her all my earnings every month. Now that you're saying I only need to give 50%, I'll actually be in a better financial position. If I had known this earlier, I would have filed for divorce five years ago!"

34. Presence of Mind

When the father returned home from the office, he was in a foul mood. Things had not gone well at work. He found his son, who was in 9th grade, looking pensive and withdrawn. The father approached him and asked, "Why so sad, son?"

"What can I say, Dad? I failed because of just one mark," the son replied.

The father felt sorry for him and said, "That's no problem, son. Sometimes, despite our best efforts, things like this happen."

In reality, the son had scored only one out of a hundred. His presence of mind helped him avoid a harsher punishment. He did get a slap when he showed his report card, but its intensity was much less than it could have been.

35. A Knot in the Sheet

At a school parent meeting, the principal emphasised the importance of parents supporting their children. She acknowledged that while most parents in the community were workers, it was crucial for them to find time to spend with their kids. However, she was surprised when one parent stood up and explained that he didn't have time to talk to his son during the week.

He left for work very early, while his son was still asleep, and returned home very late, by which time his son was already in bed. He explained that he had to work these hours to provide for his family. He also shared that not having time for his son distressed him deeply, so he tried to make up for it by giving his son a kiss every night when he arrived home. To let his son know he had been there, he would tie a knot at the tip of the sheet.

"When my son wakes up and sees the knot, he knows that his dad has been there and has kissed him. The knot is our way of communicating," he said.

The principal was moved by this unique story and was even more surprised to learn that the man's son was one of the best students in the school. This story reminds us that there are many ways to be present and communicate with others. This father found his own simple yet effective method. The most important thing is that his son perceived all his father's affection through that knot.

Sometimes we worry so much about how we communicate that we forget the main thing is to express our feelings. Simple gestures, such as a kiss and a knot in the sheet, meant much more to that son than a lot of empty gifts or apologies. It's important to care about people, but even more important that they feel our concern and affection.

For true communication, people need to "listen" to the language of our hearts, as feelings often speak louder than words. A kiss, full of pure affection, can cure a headache, soothe a scraped knee, or dispel fear of the dark. Children may not understand the meaning of many words, but they can always recognise a gesture of love, even if it's just a knot in the sheet—a knot full of affection, tenderness, and love.

"Live in such a way that when your children think of justice, love, and integrity..."

36. Letters of Gratitude!

His father told his son, who had just joined college, to write at least three letters every day to his teachers in school and thank them for their influence and effort. The boy nodded his head in agreement and wrote his first three letters – they read, "A, B, C."

37. Don't Try to Cheat an Indian Mom

Mom visits her son Kumar for dinner. Kumar lives with his roommate, Sunita. Throughout the meal, his mother couldn't help but notice how pretty Sunita was. She had long been suspicious of a relationship between the two, and this only fuelled her curiosity.

As the evening progressed, she started to wonder if there was more between Kumar and Sunita than met the eye.

Sensing his mom's thoughts, Kumar said, "I know what you must be thinking, but I assure you, Sunita and I are just apartment mates."

About a week later, Sunita approached Kumar and said, "Ever since your mother came to dinner, I haven't been able to find the silver plate. You don't suppose she took it, do you?" Kumar replied, "I doubt it, but I'll email her just to be sure."

So, he sat down and wrote:

"Dear Mother, I'm not saying that you did take the silver plate from my house, and I'm not saying that you did not take the silver plate. But the fact remains that it has been missing ever since you were here for dinner. Love, Kumar."

Several days later, Kumar received an email from his mother that read:

"Dear Son, I'm not saying that you sleep in the same room with Sunita, and I'm not saying that you do not sleep in the same room with Sunita. But the fact remains that if she were sleeping in her own bedroom, she would have found the silver plate by now under her pillow. Love, Mom."

Don't lie to your mother, especially if she is Indian!

38. Déjà Vu

English by PT sir of a school in the village:

1) There is no wind in the football...

2) I talk, he talks, why do you talk in the middle?

3. You rotate the ground four times...

4) You go and understand the tree.

5) I'll give you a clap on your cheeks...

6) Bring your parents, your mother, and especially your father...

7) Close the window, air force is coming.

8) I have two daughters, and both are girls...

9) Stand in a straight circle...

10) Don't stand in front of my back.

11) Why is "haircut" not "haircut"...?

12) Don't make noise... the principal is rotating in the corridor.

13) Why are you looking at the monkey outside the window when I'm here?

14) You have a bad habit.

15) Give me a red pen of any colour.

16) Can I have some snow in my cold drink?

17) Pick up the paper and throw it into the dustbin.

18) Both of you stand together, separately.

19) There is no tube in the air.

20) Keep quiet, the principal just passed away!!

39. Parents: Our Lifeline

That night, Susan quarrelled with her mother and stormed out of the house. On her way out, she realised she had no money, not even enough to make a phone call home.

As she walked past a noodle shop, the enticing aroma made her realise how hungry she was. She longed for a bowl of noodles but had no money.

The seller noticed her lingering near the counter and asked, "Hey, little girl, do you want to eat a bowl?"

"But... but I don't have any money," she replied shyly.

"That's okay, I'll treat you," the seller said. "Come in, I'll cook you a bowl."

A few minutes later, he brought her a steaming bowl of noodles. As she ate, Susan started to cry.

"What's wrong?" he asked.

"Nothing. I am just touched by your kindness!" Sue said as she wiped her tears. "Even a stranger gives me a bowl of noodles, but my own mother chased me out of the house after a quarrel. She is so cruel!"

The seller sighed and said, "Girl, why do you think that way? Think again. I only gave you a bowl of noodles, and you feel this way. Your mother has raised you since you were little. Why aren't you grateful and obedient to her?"

Susan was taken aback. "Why did I not think of that? A bowl of noodles from a stranger makes me feel indebted, but my mother has raised me since I was little and I have never felt the same, even a little."

On her way home, Susan thought about what she would say to her mother when she arrived. "Mom, I'm sorry. I know it was my fault. Please forgive me..."

When she reached home, she saw her mother, worried and tired from searching for her everywhere. Upon seeing Susan, her mother gently said, "Susan, come inside, honey. You must be very hungry. I cooked rice and prepared a meal. Come eat while it's still hot."

Unable to control herself any longer, Susan cried in her mother's arms.

In life, we sometimes easily appreciate the small actions of strangers but take for granted the sacrifices of our loved ones, especially our parents.

Parental love and concern are the most precious gifts we have been given since birth. Parents do not expect us to repay them for raising us, but have we ever truly appreciated or treasured their unconditional sacrifices?

40. When You Get the Man/Woman Right

The young mother was eager for a few minutes of relaxation after a long and demanding day. However, her young daughter had other plans.

"Read me a story, Mom," the little girl requested.

"Give Mommy a few minutes to relax and unwind, and then I'll be happy to read you a story," pleaded the mother.

The little girl was insistent that mommy read to her now. With a stroke of genius, the mother tore off the back page of the magazine she was reading. It contained a full-page picture of the world. As she tore it into several pieces, she asked her daughter to put the picture together and promised to read her a story afterwards. Surely this would buy her some relaxing moments.

A short time later, the little girl announced that she had finished the puzzle.

To her astonishment, the mother saw the world picture completely assembled. She asked her daughter how she managed to do it so quickly. The little girl explained that on the reverse side of the page was a picture of a man. "You see, mommy, when I got the man together, the whole world came together."

Learning: When I get the man/woman right, the world becomes right...

41. Reflections

"In ancient Japan, a monk lived. He always carried a small mirror with him wherever he went. His disciples would laugh and whisper to each other, "Our Guru is so vain; he always looks at his own reflection in the mirror!" But the monk didn't change his habit.

One day, a king came to visit the monk. As the monk was gazing into his mirror, the king was surprised and asked, "You have renounced everything, but why can't you renounce this attachment to your own reflection?"

The monk smiled and replied, "When I have a problem, I look into the mirror to see who is responsible for it. The one who appears in the mirror is the root cause of my troubles. Then, I seek a solution to the problem. If I need someone's help, I look into the mirror again, and the one who appears is the one who can solve my problem."

The monk continued, "As long as I have this mirror with me, I will never forget that I am the cause of my own problems and that I have the power to solve them. I will always be aware of my strengths and weaknesses."

The monk's words were a revelation to the king and his disciples, and they all nodded in understanding."

42. Doctor's Distress

It's a funny world in which we are living. People are bestowed with the ability to ask any question.

In a clinic, a patient went and sat in front of the doctor. "Tell me what's the problem," the doctor asked. The patient said, "You have studied MBBS; only you have to tell me what's my problem. If I tell you my problem, what is the use of your studying MBBS?" The doctor was stunned by the question but again persisted, "Please tell me your problem. I will see if I can help solve the problem for you."

Reluctantly, the patient said, "My right knee is making noise, causing pain; it's creaking sometimes." The doctor asked the patient his age. The patient replied, saying that he is 72 years old. The doctor said, "At this age, there will be creaking noise and pain, but with some precautions, weight management, and leg strengthening, things could get better.

The patient replied, "Doctor, my left knee is also 72 years old. Why isn't it making noise and causing pain?" The doctor thought, "Oh my God, why do you send such patients to me?" But he knew getting patients was becoming more difficult. The doctor sighed and placed his right hand on his heart, feeling a bit uncomfortable. The patient noticed and said, "Doctor, just seeing one patient like me is stressing you out. It's not enough to have patients; you need to have patience too. Don't worry, it's not a serious problem, you'll be alright soon."

The patient then told the doctor to ask the chaiwallah for a strong chai with some ginger, saying it would help him feel better. "By the way, order a cup of masala chai for me too. Now, doctor, what should I do to fix my right knee?"

The doctor advised, "You should walk every day for 4 km and eat less food." The patient replied, "I came here for a solution, and you're giving me more problems!"

The doctor closed his clinic early that day as his blood pressure had risen significantly.

43. Bed # 6 in ICU

A man walked up to the reception desk in a hospital and asked the receptionist, "How is Mahesh doing in bed number 6 in the ICU?" The receptionist called the ICU and inquired, "How is Mahesh in bed number 6?" After getting the answer, she hung up and cheerfully informed the man, "Mahesh in bed number 6 is doing well and is ready to be discharged. But, may I know who you are?"

The man replied, "I am Mahesh." The receptionist was bewildered and asked, "How did you get here, that too in civilian clothes?"

Mahesh explained, "The duty doctor in the ICU has been giving evasive answers. I knew I was fine but wanted to double-check. So, I changed into normal clothes and came here." With that, he returned to the ICU, changed back into his hospital gown, and lay down.

A couple of hours later, the duty doctor came in. Mahesh asked, "When can I leave the hospital? I understand I can be discharged; I don't have any issues."

The duty doctor replied, "We've learned some things about your case. You have a house, a plot, and substantial fixed deposits in banks. Who said you can be discharged?"

44. Directions and Logistics: Planning Ahead

There is a man who meticulously follows rules and regulations. Rules and regulations everywhere. On the road, in the house, inside the office, meeting statutory obligations, everything on time all the time. The major problem is that he plans and executes his plans almost too soon. For example, even before he gets a headache, he takes a tablet for that.

Once he was travelling on the highway from Mumbai to Pune on the express highway, a 6-lane wide concrete road. He left home in his car, switched on the Google Maps, reached the highway, and noticed that he had to take a left turn after 95 km. He immediately reached for the paddle switch and switched on the indicator that he was turning left. For 95 km, the indicator was on.

After travelling about 80 km, that man felt hungry and wanted to have something to eat. He located a good restaurant through Google, which was on the right side. He switched ON the indicator to the right, travelled a few km, and then took a right turn and reached the restaurant.

In another instant, this man was to travel abroad to be with his son for a month. His son said that he would be busy and requested his dad to take a cab from the airport and reach home. The father got the address and location map from his son, who lived in the US, in New York.

Just before leaving home at Mumbai airport via Frankfurt to New York, this man took his mobile and searched for 42nd Street, New York. When he stepped into the flight, there was a recorded voice inside the aircraft to put the phone in Flight Mode!

Even if the pilot had lost his way, this man would have been able to guide the flight!

45. Math Issues

"Can you help me with a word problem, Deepa?" asked Priya.

Priya continued, "If I cut a cake into three pieces, each piece will be 0.333 of the whole, correct?"

"Yes, that's right," Deepa confirmed.

Priya frowned. "But if you multiply three by 0.333, you get 0.999. So, where did the missing 0.001 go?"

Deepa laughed. "That's simple. It's on the knife!"

46. Dispute in the Tea Shop

Shyam stood in front of a tea shop, sipping his tea. A man approached him and said, "Maharaj, I'm hungry. Can you buy me a cup of tea?"

Shyam looked the man up and down and replied, "You don't look like a beggar."

The man responded, "And you don't look like a Maharaj. Do you think you do?"

He then added, "It's fine if you can't buy me tea, but remember, I'm asking for a tea, not the whole tea shop."

47. Free with the Tea

At a roadside tea shop, a man was sipping his tea when he discovered a dead bee in it. He shouted at the shopkeeper, "There's a bee in my tea!"

The shopkeeper replied, "For the 20 rupees you're paying, I can only afford to put in a bee, not a beetle."

48. Buy One, Get One Free

When sales are slow in clothing stores, we often see offers like "Buy one, get one" or "Buy two, take five." This concept extends beyond retail into real life, where certain actions come with complimentary benefits.

Buy one, get one...

When we buy "Jealousy," we get "Headache" free!

When we buy "Anger," we get "Acidity" free!

When we buy "Stress," we get "Blood Pressure" absolutely free!

When we buy "Exercise," we get "Health" free!

When we buy "Peace," good sleep is available for free.

When we buy "Love," we receive God's divine shower of grace and blessings.

When we buy "Prayers," we get "Peace of Mind" free!

When we buy "Trust" in a relationship, "Friendship" is free!

49. Obesity

The doctor advised the patient to consult a lifestyle specialist because his BMI was over 35. A BMI above twenty-five is considered obese. The lifestyle specialist then asked the patient, "Does obesity run in your family?"

The patient responded, "As a matter of fact, no one runs in our family!"

50. Who Broke Janaka's Bow?

An inspector from a state government school education department made an unannounced visit to a village school. Entering a sixth-grade classroom, he introduced himself to the teacher and asked one of the students, "Who broke Janaka's bow?"

The student, puzzled, looked around, scratched his head, and confidently replied, "Sir, I didn't break it!"

The inspector, surprised, turned to the teacher and said, "What kind of answer is that?"

The teacher responded, "Don't worry, sir. I'll ask around and let you know who broke the bow after you leave."

Perplexed, the inspector went to the headmaster and recounted the incident. The headmaster assured him, "Sir, I'll conduct an inquiry and find out who really broke the bow."

Frustrated, the inspector returned to his office and slumped in his chair. The District Education Officer (DEO) noticed his unusual demeanour and asked, "What's wrong?"

The inspector explained the situation. The DEO (District Education Officer) sighed and said, "This is your problem; you're always trying to find out who broke what. In today's world, everything is disposable. All use and throw items. Just list it as 'broken' in our inventory and move on."

The inspector was baffled by the DEO's response, finding it hard to believe that even the DEO couldn't answer such a simple question. He went home, had a strong cup of coffee, and told his wife about the day's events.

"Do you know the answer?" he asked her.

She confidently replied, "Yes, it's a simple question and I know the answer. The person who broke the bow was Anil Shetty."

The inspector, now even more confused, asked, "Who on earth is Anil Shetty?"

His wife calmly explained, "Anil Shetty broke the bow during the Ramayana play at the school auditorium last month."

From then on, the inspector avoided asking about the Ramayana in any school he visited. He realised that just because he knew the answer, he couldn't expect everyone else to know it too.

51. Inner Wealth is More Precious

A wise woman was travelling in the mountains when she found a precious stone in a stream.

The next day, she encountered a hungry traveller and generously opened her bag to share her food. The traveller noticed the precious stone and asked for it. Without hesitation, she gave it to him.

Overjoyed by his good fortune, the traveller left, knowing the stone's value could secure his future. However, a few days later, he returned the stone to the wise woman.

"I've been reflecting," he said. "I understand the worth of this stone, but I return it to you in the hope that you can give me something even more valuable. Give me what you have within you that enabled you to give me this stone."

Moral: Sometimes it's not the wealth you possess, but what's inside you that others truly need.

52. The Misunderstood Call

"Hello, Sir. I'd like to meet and talk with you. You are the father of one of my students."

The man did not understand the question, was stunned, and blabbered: "Oh my God!"

"Are you Sandy?"

"No."

"Maria?"

"No."

"Lakshmi?"

"No."

"Divya?"

"No."

"Shruthi?"

"No."

"Shika?"

"No."

The lady, confused, replies,

"Sir, I'm your son's teacher," "Please come and talk to me. He is always up to some mischief!"

53. Good Relationships Create Good Health

The last lecture focused on the mind-body connection, specifically the relationship between stress and disease.

The speaker, the head of psychiatry at a leading university, mentioned that one of the best things a man can do for his health is to be married to a woman. In contrast, one of the best things a woman can do for her health is to nurture her relationships with her girlfriends.

Initially, everyone laughed, but he was serious.

He explained that women connect with each other differently, creating support systems that help manage stress and challenging life experiences. This "girlfriend time" physically boosts serotonin levels—a neurotransmitter that helps combat depression and promotes well-being. Women often share their feelings, while men typically bond over activities and rarely discuss their emotions or personal lives in depth. Jobs? Yes. Sports? Yes. Cars? Yes. Fishing, hunting, golf? Yes. But their feelings? Rarely.

Women, on the other hand, frequently share from their hearts with their sisters and mothers, friends, which is evidently very beneficial for their health. He stated that spending time with friends is as crucial for our health as jogging or working out at a gym.

We tend to think that exercising is good for our bodies, while hanging out with friends is unproductive—not true. In fact, he said that failing to create and maintain quality personal relationships is as dangerous to our physical health as smoking! Both intra-relationship and inter-relationships.

54. Higher Living

A man residing in the fourth tower of the G wing in a residential complex sold his seventh-floor apartment and purchased another unit in the same tower and wing, but on the thirty-eighth floor.

Despite the identical layout, his friends were intrigued about the move. The man responded saying, it's "Higher living!"

55. Reading Shapes Life

Most students don't read storybooks these days. They are almost always seen with their mobile phones. My friend shared an experience he had recently when he visited his friend's house. His friend wasn't home, so he asked his friend's son for a book to read while he waited. To his surprise, the boy handed him a Physics textbook and said, "Here, Uncle, read this," before heading out to play.

Later, my friend met his friend's elder daughter. Introducing himself as her father's friend, he requested a book to pass the time. She asked, "Uncle, would you like an English book or a Tamil book?" My friend replied, "English book, please." Dutifully, she brought him an English book, but it turned out to be her class XI English grammar textbook!

Parents should instil the habit of reading storybooks in their children from an early age. While subjects in the school curriculum prepare you for a career and help you earn a living, reading storybooks in childhood, followed by books on philosophy, biographies, and various other topics, provides a broader perspective on life and living. Both are equally important.

56. The Unexpected Twist

As they were travelling by train, the woman remarked to the man, "Sir, your smile makes me want to invite you over to my place."

The man, taken aback, responded, "That's cheeky! Are you single?"

With a grin, the woman replied, "No, and I'm an orthodontist!"

57. Tooth Extraction Mishap

These days, you can find information on almost anything by simply Googling it.

A man was experiencing severe pain in his bottom right second molar tooth. The dental arrangement from behind is as follows: wisdom tooth, first molar, second molar, first premolar, second premolar, canine, incisors, and so on. He found two dental clinics near each other through Google, just three buildings apart.

At the first clinic, he received a quote: Rs 2000 for anaesthesia and extraction. He asked for a breakdown, and the receptionist explained it was Rs 500 for anaesthesia and Rs 1500 for the extraction.

He then visited the second clinic for a competitive quote. They provided the same breakdown: Rs 500 for anaesthesia and Rs 1500 for extraction, with no discounts.

Trying to save money, he scheduled an appointment with the first dentist for 7 pm and with the second dentist for 7:15 pm on the same day.

On the appointed day, he went to the first clinic at 7 pm, got the anaesthesia injection, and told the doctor he would wait outside for 15 minutes. He then walked to the second clinic at 7:15 pm and asked the dentist to remove his tooth. When the dentist instructed the nurse to prepare the anaesthesia injection, the patient insisted it wasn't needed, claiming he could bear the pain.

Despite the dentist's advice, the patient refused anaesthesia. He pointed out the tooth to be extracted, and the dentist removed it. Both the doctor and nurse were surprised he didn't show any pain.

After examining the extracted tooth, the dentist remarked, "This tooth looks fine. Why did you want it removed?" The patient pointed again to the painful second molar, but the dentist had removed the premolar by mistake. Shocked, the patient exclaimed, "Doctor, I showed you this tooth, but you removed the adjacent one!"

After some argument, the dentist gave him an anaesthetic injection and extracted the correct tooth. His bill came to Rs. 1500 for the incorrect extraction and Rs. 2000 for the correct one, totalling Rs. 3500.

Meanwhile, the first dentist was left waiting for his patient who had never returned.

58. Priorities

The speaker, speaking about philosophy, captivated the audience with his phenomenal insights, wit, wisdom, and communication. After half an hour into his talk, someone opened the adjacent kitchen door where evening snacks like pakora, sweets with ghee were being made.

The vapour of ghee and the vapour of gingelly oil while making the sweet and pakora got mixed, and the smell of vapour captured the sensory stimuli of smell and communicated it to the mind. Now the attention was on "when the speaker would finish his talk so that they could have their sweets and pakora!"

It's all about priorities! As they say, "When the stomach is hungry, philosophy goes to the dogs!"

59. Burial Request

There was a wealthy elderly man who was extremely possessive of his new car. His admiration for it was so great that he visited his lawyer to draft his will. It stated, "All my possessions, including property, stocks, cash, and other valuables, will be bequeathed to my only son; however, my car must be buried with me when I die."

Request to son: Dear son, please ensure that the car is filled with petrol before you bury it along with my body, as I'm not sure if petrol will be available at the destination where I am going to!

60. First Time Lessons

This happened more than four decades ago when I was in my first year of engineering. One day, after returning my classmate's laboratory record book at his house, I was biking home and got stopped by a policeman. When I asked him what the problem was, he informed me that I was riding my bicycle in a "No Entry" zone. I explained that I thought one-way traffic rules applied only to motorised vehicles, but he insisted that I leave my bicycle there and collect it the following day from the police station with an apology letter.

I went straight to my uncle, a very senior police officer at HQ. After a 15-minute wait, I explained the situation to him, expecting his help. Instead, he became very angry and shouted, "If you had murdered someone, raped someone, or stolen something, I might have tried to help you. But for a petty offence like riding a bicycle the wrong way and coming to me for help? Get lost."

Feeling dejected, I went home with a sullen face and couldn't sleep that night. The next day, I wrote an apology letter, went to the police station, and retrieved my bicycle. Since then, I've never gone the wrong way on a one-way street.

The best thing that can happen to someone early in life is to be punished the very first time they do something wrong. It taught me a valuable lesson—so much so that even when walking on a "one-way" street, I'm cautious.

61. Once Too Often

My uncle passed away at the age of ninety-eight. As the hearse van carried his body to the cremation ground, I followed in my car. Our relative, who was at his house, had asked me to call him when we were nearing the cremation ground so he could join us for the final rites. I called him, and he joined us as planned.

Two months later, my aunt, the wife of the uncle who had passed away, also passed away at the age of ninety. Following the same pattern, I drove behind the hearse van and called our relative when we were nearing the cremation ground. He told me, "This time, I'm not coming."

It felt as though these events were happening so frequently that one could afford to skip some and attend others.

62. Height of Embarrassment

Someone described the height of embarrassment as peeping through a keyhole to see what's happening on the other side, only to find another eye staring back at you just as curiously!

63. Reversal of Hairstyle: Tradition in India

Women's hairstyles in urban areas in India have evolved considerably over the years. In the past, women often wore their hair in plaits and used clips to keep it tidy when going out, while at home, they would let their hair down to relax. This trend has since reversed. Nowadays, with the availability of various haircuts, including different lengths, straightening, perming, colouring, and streaking, women typically prefer to leave their hair loose when they are outside and use bands to tie it up when they are at home.

64. Children and Their Understanding of Family Dynamics

Mayank and Shika were classmates and neighbours, both in the second grade and seven years old. Watching too much television and serials had made an indelible impression on their young minds.

One Sunday, Mayank went to Shika's home. Both Shika and Mayank were playing "Family game." At that time, Shika's father came along. Mayank met Shika's father and asked for Shika's hand in marriage. Stunned, Shika's father gathered himself and asked, "How will you run the family? Don't you need money?"

Mayank confidently replied, "I get Rs 100 per month as pocket money, and Shika told me she gets Rs 200 per month. With that, I think we can live our life."

Shika's father then asked, "Where will you stay?"

Mayank answered, "My room in our house is quite big, and we both could live there."

Finding the conversation increasingly surreal, Shika's father asked, "What if some children come along?"

Mayank responded, "We've been lucky so far not to have any yet!"

65. A Nostalgic Tale from 50 Years Ago

About 50 years ago, owning a bicycle was a significant achievement for a middle-class family. During that time, it was mandatory to have a light on a bicycle after dark. Police would fine those who rode without one. Cyclists typically used a dynamo light or a wick lamp, not so much to illuminate the road, but to signal their presence to others coming from the opposite side.

One evening, a man was riding his bicycle without a light. A policeman stopped him and was about to fine him. The cyclist argued, "There are streetlights everywhere; why do I need a light?"

In response, the policeman bent down and let the air out of the rear tyre with a hiss.

The cyclist, bewildered, exclaimed, "What are you doing? Why did you remove the air? Who will fill it up?"

The policeman calmly replied, "The street is filled with air, so you can fill it up as much as you wish!"

66. Smart Answer

"How far are you from the right answer?" the teacher asked the student sitting at the back during a surprise test. The student counted and replied, "Sir, four tables!"

67. Neighbourly Insurance Connection

My uncle and aunt migrated to the UK about four decades ago with their family. My aunt worked in the insurance department. They lived in one of the twin homes, which is owned by two independent people and physically separated by a common wall.

Unlike in India, people in the West often do not know their neighbours even after decades. One day, my aunt, who worked in the claims department of the insurance company, came across a claim from a widow. She checked the name, insurance date, validity, amount, premium payments, and the address. To her surprise, it was her own address! She double-checked, thinking it might be a mistake, but then realised it could be the family living on the other side of the common wall.

To confirm, she called the widow and verified that she indeed lived next door. Yes, the woman had passed away recently. My aunt introduced herself as her neighbour, sharing the same wall, and offered her condolences. "So near, yet so far," my aunt mused.

68. Avian Artistry

There are two ways to reach our home, both lined with large avenue trees on either side. One road is wider, so the branches from the trees don't touch each other. On the narrower road, however, the branches from both sides interlace. Even during peak summer, this road provides complete shade.

The trees are fine, but the crows nesting in their branches create a mess. Their droppings scatter across the road, making it look like a modern art exhibit titled "Poop on Tar." The smell, especially after a hot day, is quite unpleasant.

When I ride my bike, I take the narrower road, and when driving the car, I use the wider road. There's no particular reason for this choice; it's just a preference. However, I avoid the narrower road after 6 pm because that's when the crows return to their nests. When a two-wheeler with its headlight on passes by, the crows seem to calculate the bike's speed, distance, and angle, then drop their droppings with precise accuracy, rarely missing their target.

Once I tried and successfully rode through the less wide road after 6 pm. I turned off the light. The crows could not see a bike in darkness. We talk about laser-guided bombs and missiles, but it makes me think their inspiration might have come from observing crows.

69. Unexpected Realisations

Dinesh, the father of a 3-year-old, was a busy man. He travelled frequently and spent weekends working from home. His wife often complained, but his demanding corporate job left him little choice. Despite being well-compensated, family time had become a secondary priority.

One Saturday, a get-together was arranged, bringing many of his corporate colleagues, along with their wives and children, to a dinner party on the lawns of a five-star hotel. With an abundance of food and lively conversation, everyone enjoyed the evening.

During the gathering, families began discussing their children, all of whom were between the ages of 3 and 6. Proudly, Dinesh called his son over and sweetly asked, "Out of all the people in the world, whom do you like the most?" expecting the answer to be "Daddy."

To his surprise, his son replied, "Mommy." Everyone laughed and nodded in agreement. Dinesh continued, "Next, whom do you like the most?" His son said, "Grandfather." "Next?" Dinesh asked. "Grandmother," his son replied. Growing frustrated, Dinesh finally asked, "So, what ranking would you give me in the order of your preferences?"

Much to his dismay and embarrassment, his son replied, "42nd!"

The lesson here is: Quality time equals love in a relationship, while time equals money in business.

70. Humorous Encounter at a Southern Indian Wedding

For women living in southern India about 50 years ago, "north India" referred to anything north of Chennai, encompassing cities like Bombay, Delhi, and Calcutta. At a wedding, families from Bombay, Delhi, and Calcutta were introduced to an elderly woman who had never travelled north of Madras.

Upon meeting them, the old woman innocently asked, "You said that you all live in North India. Do you meet quite often?" unaware of the vast distances between the cities.

71. Texting Codes

Since the younger generation has its own texting codes (LOL, OMG, TTYL, etc.), the older folks decided not to be left behind and created their own set of codes:

- ATD: At the Doctor's

- BFF: Best Friend's Funeral

- BTW: Bring the Wheelchair

- BYOT: Bring Your Own Teeth

- FWIW: Forgot Where I Was

- GGPBL: Gotta Go, Pacemaker Battery Low

- GHA: Got Heartburn Again

- TFT: Texting from the Toilet

- TTYL: Try to Yawn Less

- FOMO: Full of Medical Opinions

72. The Older I Get...

I've changed my car horn to sound like gunshots. People move out of the way much faster now!

Gone are the days when girls used to cook like their mothers; now they drink like their fathers.

I didn't make it to the gym today. That makes five years in a row.

I've decided to stop calling the bathroom the "John" and renamed it the "Jim." Now, I feel so much better saying, "I went to the Jim this morning."

Old age is coming at a really bad time. When I was a child, I thought "nap time" was a punishment. Now, as an adult, it feels like a mini-vacation.

The biggest lie I tell myself is, "I don't need to write that down; I'll remember it."

I don't have grey hair; I have "wisdom highlights." I'm just very wise.

Don't ever ask me to bend down and touch my toes. If God wanted me to touch my toes, He would have put them on my knees.

Last year, I joined a support group for procrastinators. We haven't met yet.

Of course, I talk to myself; sometimes I need expert advice.

At my age, "getting lucky" means walking into a room and remembering why I came in there.

Actually, I'm not complaining because I am a "senager" (senior teenager).

I have everything I wanted as a teenager, only 60 years later:

- I don't have to go to school or work.

- I have a driver's licence and my own car.

- I get an allowance every month.

- I have my own iPad (though I can't remember where I put it).

- I don't have a curfew.

Life is great.

I have more friends I should send this to, but right now I can't remember their names.

Now I'm wondering... did I send this to you, or did you send it to me?

73. Not Easy Being a Teacher

Teacher: "Construct a sentence using the word 'sugar'."

Student: "I drank tea this morning."

Teacher: "Where is the word 'sugar'?"

Student: "It's already in the tea!"

Teacher: "Our topic for today is photosynthesis."

Teacher: "Class, what is photosynthesis?"

Student: "Photosynthesis is our topic for today."

Teacher: "John is climbing a tree to pick some mangoes. Start the sentence with 'Mangoes.'"

Student: "Mangoes, John is coming to pick you..."

Teacher: "What do you call mosquitoes in your language?"

Student: "We don't call them; they come on their own..."

Teacher: "Name the nation people hate most."

Student: "Examination."

Teacher: "How can we keep our school clean?"

Student: "By staying at home..."

Teacher: "One day our country will be corruption-free. What tense is that?"

Student: "Future impossible tense..."

Dedicated to all naughty ex-students!

74. Flight Delay

A man called the travel office, upset that the cab he had ordered to take him to the airport for his flight to Mumbai hadn't arrived. The receptionist, a young woman, replied, "Sir, I'm very sorry, but your cab is still on its way. But don't worry, I just checked, the plane is also delayed." The man responded sharply, "Young lady, I happen to be the pilot!"

75. Fast Food and Combo

Fast food came into this world in the year 1916 in Kansas. It made its debut in India at New Delhi in 1977. Fast food is the name given to preparing food quickly and inexpensively and suitable for people who are on the move; moreover, it is tasty and doesn't pinch the wallet that much.

These days, fast food comes in combos. If one buys mutton biryani, five pieces of chicken sixty-five are given for free; this, apart from half a litre of some form of carbonated drink included in the package. However, it is not mentioned that "heart attacks also come in for free!"

Non-vegetarian food can be high in protein and fat, which may be difficult to digest when paired with a carbonated drink, unless taken in moderation.

76. Invisible Struggles

While driving, I encountered a car moving slowly and not giving way despite my persistent honking. I was about to lose my temper when I noticed a small sticker on the rear of the car: "Physically challenged; Please be patient."

Suddenly, everything changed. I calmed down and slowed my pace. In fact, I felt protective of the car and its driver. I reached home a few minutes late, but it was okay.

This experience made me think: Would I have been as patient if there hadn't been a sticker? Why do we need such reminders to be patient with others? What if people had labels on their foreheads indicating their struggles, like:

"Lost my job,"

"Fighting cancer,"

"Going through a bad divorce,"

"Suffering emotional abuse,"

"Lost a loved one,"

"Feeling worthless,"

"Financially broken."

Everyone is fighting their own battles and wars that we know nothing about. The least we can do is be patient, kind, and compassionate. Let's respect the invisible labels each person carries.

That's why it's said: Walk gently into others' lives; not all wounds are visible.

77. A Letter in Perception

It was the final exam for the psychology students before they would receive their degrees. The eccentric psychology professor entered the exam hall and announced, "Take down this question and answer it within one hour." He then wrote the question on the whiteboard: "Using everything we've learned this semester, prove that this chair does not exist."

The students scratched their heads, trying to recall everything they had been taught. They feverishly wrote down all the theories, axioms, and concepts they knew, attempting to prove that the chair did not exist. However, they were surprised when one student quickly wrote something down and left the classroom within five minutes.

The rest of the class continued to write, filling extra sheets with their arguments. When the results were announced, the students were astonished to see that the student who had handed in their paper after just five minutes had received an "A," while no one else scored higher than a "C."

Curious, the students asked to see the answer paper of the student who had received the "A." The professor showed it to them: it simply read, "What chair!?"

78. Navigational Standoff

This happened on a dark stormy night. The Communication Department in a ship received an internal call from the Navigation Department while at sea. They were instructed to inform an approaching light to change course by 20 degrees. They did not know whether it was a cargo ship or a passenger ship.

The communication between them went as follows:

Ship's Communication Department: "This is a call from the ship. Please move 20 degrees north. Stay clear of our course."

Response: "If you want, you should move."

Ship's Navigation Department: "Sir, move 20 degrees north immediately, or you will be smashed to pieces."

Response: "If you want to avoid a collision, you should change course. It's for your own good."

Ship's Executive Officer: "Hello, seaman. Please move 20 degrees north, or you will suffer the consequences."

Response: "Sir, with all due respect, you should move quickly and avoid the crash."

Ship's Commanding Officer: "Why won't you move? This is a warship, and you're playing games with us. Who are you? Are you a pirate ship?"

Response: "Sir, I politely inform you that I am in the lighthouse! It seems your navigation system isn't working properly."

79. Mind Matters

According to reports, in western and developed countries, four out of every five people go and see a psychiatrist. The fifth person is a psychiatrist!

80. Understanding the Processes

A man went to a bank to transfer his money to another bank. He wrote a cheque, handed it to the officer at the counter, and asked, "How long will it take for the money to be transferred?" The officer replied, "It will take about 48 hours."

The man pleaded, "Sir, the branch of the bank I am transferring the money to is just across the road. Can't you transfer it immediately?" The officer patiently explained, "Sir, there are certain formalities, procedures, protocols that have to be followed."

The customer became insistent, saying, "If you really want to help, you can do it."

The officer responded, "Let me explain it with an example. Suppose you're walking home and, unfortunately, you pass away near a burial ground. Would they bury your body there immediately, or would they take it home, perform the rituals, and then bring it back for burial?"

The customer answered, "Of course, they would take the body home, follow the proper procedures and rituals before the burial."

The officer said, "Similarly, the check you deposited needs to go through certain procedures and formalities before the funds can be transferred to the other bank. I hope that clears it up."

The customer nodded in understanding.

81. Stock Market Advisory

Investor: How to make Rs 1 crore in the stock market?

Stock market adviser: Start with Rs 2 crore.

82. Problem-solving in Interviews

A journalist, a social worker, and a lawyer are being interviewed for a management position in a large corporate division. The journalist is called in first. He sits down and faces a panel of stern-faced interviewers.

They start with questions about his experience, qualifications, and previous work. Finally, the head interviewer, with a serious expression, asks, "How much is two plus two?" The journalist furrows his brow, thinks deeply, and then confidently responds, "Twenty-two?" The interviewers exchange glances and thank him for his time, inviting the next candidate, the social worker, to enter the room.

The social worker takes a seat and is greeted with the same set of questions. She answers each one thoughtfully, discussing her background, approach to problem-solving, and passion for helping others. The interviewers seem impressed, but then they come to the final question, "How much is two plus two?" The social worker pauses, reflects on the question, and finally says, "I don't know the answer, but I'm very glad we had the opportunity to discuss it." The interviewers nod politely, thank her for her response, and usher her out.

Finally, it's the lawyer's turn. He strides in confidently and takes a seat. The interviewers ask the same questions, and the lawyer responds with sharp, precise answers. The interviewers are intrigued by his assertiveness and legal acumen.

Then comes the last question, "How much is two plus two?" Leaning across the desk, the lawyer replies in a low voice, "How much do you want it to be?"

83. The True Measure of Wealth

Who is truly rich, and who is truly poor? This distinction reveals a profound truth about our understanding of wealth. Many believe that richness and poverty are defined by quantity—more money, more success. They think, "If I just acquire that amount, I'll be wealthy." But that's not the essence of true richness.

Real wealth lies in the relationship between what you desire and what you possess. If your desires exceed your wealth, you are, in truth, poor. Conversely, if your desires are in harmony with your wealth, then you are rich. It's not about the figures; it's about balance.

84. Customer is Always Right

The supermarket manager was advising a new recruit on proper conduct, emphasising politeness, helpfulness, and honesty with customers. He said, "Always remember, the customer is the king and they are always right!"

Eager to impress the manager, the new recruit did his best. However, the next day, the manager noticed that customers were speaking briefly with the recruit and then leaving quickly. Concerned, he wanted to find out why and address the issue.

The manager called the recruit and asked, "What have you been telling the customers?" The recruit replied, "Sir, the customers were satisfied with the products but felt the prices were too high. They asked if I agreed."

The recruit continued, "Sir, you told me that the customer is always right. So, whenever they said the prices were high, I agreed and told them, 'You are absolutely right!'"

85. The Nature of Happiness

Happiness is like a butterfly. When we go in search of the butterfly, trying to catch it, it evades us easily. But when we are focused on what we do intently, the butterfly comes and sits on our shoulder.

We do everything for getting happiness, not understanding that we should do everything out of happiness. The world is always in a state of flux, ever changing. When we chase one desire, another one would crop up; more and more desires will crop up. The first law in economics says that, "wants are many but the means of satisfying them are limited."

Even if we have sufficient resources to get objects of our liking, it can never ever leave a lasting happiness in us. The goal posts in the world of objects would keep changing.

However, there are a few things that can give us lasting happiness. They are:

1. To be grateful. An attitude of gratitude. Things could have been far worse. To count our blessings and not our troubles.

2. The Law of the Universe says that, "As you give, you will receive." So, if we need anything from the world, we should first "Give."

3. Living in the Present Moment.

These three axioms are very important to live a life of sustained happiness.

86. Why Some Men Prefer to Watch Football in Pubs or Cafés

Wife: Where are you off to?

Husband: I'm going to watch the game at the pub.

Wife: Why don't you watch it here with me?

Husband: I want to watch it with my friends.

Wife: So, I don't matter to you?

Husband: Alright, I'll stay.

Wife: Why is the goalkeeper wearing black?

Husband: He's mourning his mother.

Wife: How does the commentator know all the players' names?

Husband: It's his job.

Wife: There's a goal!

Husband: No, that's offside.

Wife: What's offside?

Husband: No, just kidding, it's a goal.

Wife: Seriously, what is offside?

Husband: Offside is the name of the coach.

Wife: Where's the coach, then?

Husband: He's on the sidelines.

Wife: Why isn't he playing?

Husband: He doesn't play; he manages the players and strategies.

Wife: Is Maradona playing?

Husband: No, he passed away.

Wife: Oh my God, how?

Husband: He watched a game with his wife.

87. The Law of the Seed

Imagine an apple tree with five hundred apples, each containing ten seeds. That's a lot of seeds, and one might wonder, "Why so many for just a few more trees?" Nature is teaching us a lesson here: most seeds won't grow. If you want to achieve something, you need to try multiple times.

This principle applies in life:

- You might need to attend twenty interviews to get one job.

- You might interview forty people to find one good employee.

- You might talk to fifty people to sell one house, car, vacuum cleaner, insurance policy, or idea.

- You might meet a hundred acquaintances to find one special friend.

Understanding the "Law of the Seed" helps us avoid disappointment. We stop feeling like victims and recognise that nature's laws are not personal. Instead, we just need to understand and work with them.

Summary:

Successful people often fail more because they plant more seeds.

When Things Are Beyond Your Control

For constant misery, follow this recipe:

a) Decide how the world *should* be.

b) Make rules for how everyone *should* behave.

When reality doesn't match your rules, you'll be angry and miserable!

For example, you might expect:

- Friends to return favours. One should remember that feedback is never given, even when asked for! Forget favours!

- People to appreciate you.

- Planes to arrive on time.

- Everyone, be honest.

These expectations seem reasonable, but often they won't be met, leaving you frustrated and disappointed.

Instead, try a better strategy: have fewer demands and more preferences. For things beyond your control, think: "I would prefer 'A,' but if 'B' happens, it's okay too." This mental shift can bring more peace of mind.

You might prefer people to be polite, but if they're rude, it doesn't ruin your day. You might prefer sunshine, but rain is okay too.

To become happier, we can either:

a) Change the world, or

b) Change our thinking. The latter is easier!

In a Nutshell:

It's not what happens to you that determines your happiness, but how you think about what happens.

Everything will be okay in the end. If it's not okay, it's not the end.

88. Funeral Services: Competition

I was having tea at a roadside teashop when I overheard a conversation between two other customers. One mentioned that he had to take the body of a young boy to the burial ground, while the other said he had to take the body of an elderly woman to the cremation ground. They discussed death as if it were a routine topic, which caught my attention. Noticing my interest, one of them asked if I lived nearby. I replied, "No," and inquired about their conversation.

The man explained that they were both in the funeral service business, transporting the deceased to burial or cremation grounds. They both owned hearse vans and provided freezer boxes, even arranging for last rites. He handed me his business card, saying, "Sir, please call me for quality service." Not wanting to be left out, the other person also gave me his card and added, "Sir, we offer funeral services at competitive rates. You can call us even if someone is in critical condition, and we'll prepare the freezer box."

After taking their cards and paying for my tea, I hurried back to the nearby site where we were working. There, I tore their business cards and threw them into two separate bins, thinking at least there would be no competition or rivalry between the cards!

89. Bridging the Gap Between Knowledge and Implementation

We go to religious places, hear spiritual discourses in person, through social media, watch a lot of YouTube videos talking about health, wealth, relationships, handling emotions, financial freedom, practising gratitude, the gift of giving, being in the present moment, following morals and ethics, and so on...

Our memories have a preferential dementia! While we know all the good things said are good, we forget what we have learned. An ounce of implementation is better than gallons of hearing.

Everyone can appreciate the good, but not everyone can stay with the good!

90. A Matter of Respect

Clerk in government office tells his officer: Sir, this is too much. The minister is shouting at me for everything, even though I manage to do my best under the circumstances.

Officer: That's all right. Please don't take it to heart. Take it easy.

Clerk: My point is simple, sir. How can a temporary employee shout at a permanent employee!?

91. Destiny vs Free Will

Student: Master, is there such a thing as destiny?

Master: The answer is both yes and no.

Student: What's the difference between destiny and free will?

Master: Think of it this way: by the time you're 21, your height is determined—that's your destiny. But your weight, from that point on, is largely within your control—that's your free will! Remember, you are the creator of your own destiny, and your choices can shape it.

92. A Priceless Run

A miser is someone who avoids spending money, even on themselves! After work, a miser waited for the bus to take him home. When the bus arrived, he chose not to board it. Instead, he ran behind the bus all the way to his destination. Upon reaching home, he proudly told his wife that he had saved Rs 5 by not taking the bus. His wife, with a hint of sarcasm, replied, "You should have run behind a taxi; you could have saved Rs 100!"

93. The Spectrum of Laughter

The amount of laughter we share varies greatly depending on the context, the situation, and the person involved. For example, in front of our boss or higher-ups, we tend to laugh heartily, often even at their less-than-smart jokes! With subordinates, we keep our laughter to a minimum, trying to emphasise the seriousness of work. Among friends, laughter flows freely and without restraint for any and all occasions. When it comes to our wives, we laugh when they're right and we're wrong, but hold back when they make a mistake. With our fathers, laughter is rare, while with our mothers, it's more measured. And with our husbands, we tend to laugh only when they're in the wrong.

94. Defying Expectations: The Bumblebee Mindset

We all have a limited "bandwidth" of perception, shaping what we believe is possible. The life you experience is constrained by this bandwidth, even though you are inherently capable of limitless possibilities. Research indicates that before the age of 14, a child hears "you can't" an average of 148,000 times. The intention behind these warnings may be protective, like stopping a child from climbing a table or using a knife to prevent injury. However, the cumulative effect is that by the time we reach 14, we've internalised this message from parents, teachers, peers, and society—resulting in a constant internal echo of "you can't."

It's remarkable that anyone achieves anything in life given this conditioning. When faced with a new challenge, this internal voice, amplified by the voices of others, often tells us it's impossible. For instance, if ten people around you, each influenced by these 148,000 "you can'ts," advise against doing something, it becomes even harder to believe you can.

This conditioning is similar to the scientific conclusion that a bumblebee shouldn't be able to fly because its wings are too small for its body size. However, the bumblebee doesn't know this and continues to fly, defying expectations. Unlike the bumblebee, humans can be conditioned by others to believe they can't do something.

To break free from these limitations, we must expand our perception bandwidth and believe in our potential. We need to renew our self-perception and adopt the mindset that "you can."

95. What's in Your Cup?

You are holding a cup of coffee when someone comes along and bumps into you or shakes your arm, causing you to spill your coffee everywhere.

Why did you spill the coffee?

"Because someone bumped into me!"

Wrong answer. You spilled the coffee because there was coffee in your cup. If there had been tea in the cup, you would have spilled tea. Whatever is inside the cup is what will spill out.

Similarly, when life shakes you (and it will), whatever is inside you will come out. It's easy to pretend until you get rattled. So, we have to ask ourselves, "What's in my cup?"

When life gets tough, what spills over?

Is it joy, gratitude, peace, and humility? Or is it anger, bitterness, a victim mentality, and a tendency to quit?

Life provides the cup, but you choose how to fill it.

Today, let's work towards filling our cups with gratitude, forgiveness, joy, words of affirmation, resilience, positivity, kindness, gentleness, and love for others.

96. A Search for Meaning

Man: "Alexa, what is the meaning of life? What is the purpose of life?"

Alexa: "The nearest liquor store is one kilometre away."

97. You are a Product of the Environment

Tell me your friends and I will tell you who you are is a famous adage. Extrapolating this statement, one could deduce that:

If you hang around with five confident people, you could well be the sixth.

If you hang around with five millionaires, you could well be the sixth.

If you hang around with five intelligent people, you could become an intelligent person yourself.

If you hang around with 5 humourists, you could become a humourist.

If you hang around with five thieves, you could become the sixth.

If you hang around with five selfless people, you could become a selfless person.

If you hang around with five selfish people, you could become the sixth selfish person.

Come back from a rose garden after staying there long enough, and you will come back smelling as roses.

This is an eternal formula. The formula does not care where it is applied, but wherever it is applied, one could reasonably expect the outcome as a product of the environment; the maximum time you spend your time with.

Buddha says: Sangam Saranam Gacchami. Meaning – "I go to the Sangha for Refuge."

98. Multi-tasking

Barking dogs don't bite (when they are barking!)

The reason: Dogs don't know multitasking!

99. The Raven's Journey to Self-acceptance

This story is for those who are dissatisfied with their lives and believe others are happier.

Once upon a time, a raven was very unhappy with his life. One day, while sitting on a tree branch, he started crying. A monk was sitting on the same tree. A drop of the raven's tears fell on the monk's cheek. The monk looked up and saw the crying raven. He asked, "What's the matter, my friend? Why are you crying?" The raven replied, "Oh wise one, I am very upset with my life. No one loves me; people shoo me away in disgrace. No one gives me anything to eat; everyone hates me. Death is better than such a life."

The monk's heart filled with compassion. He said, "My friend, we should learn to be happy in whatever condition we are in." But the raven did not understand the monk's wisdom and kept crying. The monk then said, "Don't be upset. Tell me, what do you want to be? I can make you that with my mantra." The raven became happy and said, "Oh blessed one, if you want to do me a favour, please make me a swan." The monk agreed but asked the raven to first check with the swan to see if he was happy with his life.

The raven happily flew away to meet the swan. He saw a swan swimming in a pond. He said to the swan, "How beautiful you are, as white as milk. Everyone loves you. You must be the happiest bird in the world." The swan replied sadly, "No, my friend, I am not happy. There are so many beautiful colours in the world, but I am only white, which is no colour at all. I think the parrot must be the happiest bird in the world. He is so colourful."

The raven then flew to the parrot and said, "Oh parrot, you are so colourful and beautiful. You must be the happiest bird in the world." The parrot replied sadly, "No, my friend, I am not happy. People keep parrots in cages. I am always afraid someone will catch me and lock me up. I think the peacock is the happiest bird in the world. He is much more colourful than me."

Hearing this, the raven searched for a peacock. After a long search, he found one in a zoo, where hundreds of people had gathered to see him. After the people left, the raven approached the peacock and said, "Dear peacock, you are so beautiful. Every day, thousands of people come to see you. When people see me, they immediately shoo me away. You must be the happiest bird on the planet." The peacock replied sadly, "I always thought I was the most beautiful and happy bird on the planet. But because of my beauty, I am trapped in this zoo. When people pluck my colourful feathers to make decorative items, it hurts me a lot. I am not happy, my friend."

Surprised, the raven asked, "If you are not happy, then who do you think is the happiest bird in the world?"

The peacock said, "I have examined the zoo carefully and realised that you, the raven, are the only bird not kept in a cage. People don't try to catch you and lock you up. For the past few days, I have been thinking that if I were a raven, I could happily roam everywhere and be free."

Hearing this, the raven flew away. For the first time, he felt happy to be a raven. He returned to the sage and said, "Oh wise one, I do not want to be anything else. I am fine as I am."

If we look at our lives, we find this is our problem too. We compare ourselves to others and become sad, cursing our own lives.

We overlook what we have, leading to a cycle of unhappiness.

You should learn to be happy with what you have instead of focusing on what you don't.

There will always be someone who has more or less than you.

If you keep comparing yourself to others, you will never be happy.

A person who is satisfied with what they have is the happiest person in the world.

100. Success Isn't a Name Game

It's difficult to understand why people believe there is a shortcut to success. I met a father whose son had just received his board exam results. The son had good marks but not enough to secure a seat in a medical college. The father mentioned that he didn't listen to his friend, who had advised him to change his son's name from Deepak to Deepak. He believed that if he had changed the name, his son would have scored higher and secured a medical college seat.

While luck, or "grace" in a spiritual context, can play a role, it alone is insufficient. Success requires hours of preparation, confidence, understanding the questions, and answering them in a way that maximises marks. Combining hard work with a bit of grace can lead to better results. Despite his son's marks, he can still succeed in life by pursuing another course or trying again.

The main issue here is the superstition behind changing names. Does it work? There's a limit to everything. Another friend of mine sought help from a nameologist because he was facing constant failures. Their conversation went like this:

My friend: Sir, can you suggest a remedy to fix my bad luck? I seem to be failing everywhere.

Nameologist: What is your name, sir?

My friend: My name is Srinivasan.

Nameologist: (After making some calculations) Your name seems fine. What are your initials?

My friend: My initial is R. Srinivasan.

Nameologist: Hmm... now I see the problem. The issue is with your initial. Change it from R to M or N, and you will attract all the luck.

My friend was stunned, paid the nameologist, went home, and started analysing the causes of his recurrent failures. He identified a pattern, studied the cause, corrected the causes, and eventually achieved the results he desired.

Studying the cause, a journey of effort and grace outshines superstition!

101. Internship in Handling Life

The best internship a parent could provide for understanding life involves sending their son or daughter for a brief experience of 1-2 days or more in the following settings:

1. An emergency room in a government hospital. (Life is just a flicker. In one moment, things could change and land you in the hospital. Witnessing how quickly things can change.)

2. A call centre (Experiencing frequent negative or rude interactions).

3. A cancer hospital (Observing struggle, hope, faith, prayer, and blessings).

4. Outside a mortuary (Learning about impermanence, the value of time, resilience, relationships, health, and coping with grief).

5. In a cemetery (Understanding the inevitability of our return ticket).

6. Outside an ICU (Seeing medical advancements, hope, prayer, and faith at work).

7. With a child under 3 years old (Learning about innocence and its gradual loss).

8. With an elderly couple over 85 years old (Gaining insights into relationships, complementing each other, and life's uncertainties).

9. With a childless couple married for about 25 years (Understanding sadness, frustration, anger, societal pressure, acceptance, and maintaining positivity).

10. With a farmer on their farm (Learning about process and patience).

11. In a police station (Witnessing the variety of complaints, abuses, and apathy reported).

12. In a prison (Experiencing the lack of freedom).

13. In a corporate office (Learning about efficiency, productivity, customer/client focus, leadership and management, team dynamics, and financial acumen).

14. In a government office (Understanding public service, ethics, stability, job security, community impact, and policy regulation).

15. On a construction site (learning building techniques, using tools and equipment, reading blueprints, project management, safety, and time management).

Life has to be experienced holistically. Life is wholesome.

102. The Power of Words

Words have tremendous power to make you or break you. They can inspire, encourage, and build someone up, or they can hurt, discourage, and tear someone down. The impact of words can be profound and long-lasting, affecting self-esteem, relationships, and overall well-being. This is why it's important to choose our words carefully and use them with kindness and empathy.

Once, a father saw his 4-year-old son scribbling on the wall with a crayon. He shouted, "Hey, stop it! Don't scribble on the wall again." Did the boy stop? No, he used more colours to scribble and extended his artwork to the adjacent walls too!

When the father returned a few minutes later, his son looked at him and continued scribbling. The father, now wiser, said, "Sweetie, you're a big boy now; big boys don't scribble on the walls." The son looked at his dad, nodded, and said, "Yes, big boys don't do such things." He then put the crayons away and went out to play. His pride was lifted, and he now had a reputation to uphold.

In another instance, the son, now grown up, expected his father to acknowledge and praise him. He accomplished many things, but his father never appreciated nor acknowledged his achievements. Once, he received four straight A's at university and thought this achievement would finally earn his father's acknowledgement and appreciation.

He called his dad and said, "Dad, I got four straight A's." Instead of appreciating his son's achievement, the dad replied that he was busy and to call him later. The son was shattered by his father's apathy. He turned to alcohol and drugs and never recovered.

The power of words is immense and multifaceted. They can inspire, heal, persuade, and unite, but they can also harm, deceive, and divide. Some key aspects of the power of words: They can influence, motivate, have an emotional impact and heal. The power of words lies in their ability to shape our reality. They can build bridges or walls, empower or demoralise. As such, it's important to use words thoughtfully and responsibly.

103. The Need for Appreciation

One of the fundamental principles of human nature is the craving for acknowledgement and appreciation. Just as the sun, soil, and water are essential for human survival, praise and appreciation are vital for hope and inspiration. This need applies to all of us. In fact, next to physical survival, the greatest need of a human being is psychological survival and the deep yearning to be appreciated.

A sincere compliment, acknowledgement, appreciation, or praise has propelled many to achieve great success. Most people enjoy the warm feeling that comes when we are made to feel special—when we know that we matter. When we feel valued and connected, we become more energised, productive, and perform our best work. All of us want to know that we make a difference. When family members are engaged, there is harmony in the family. Similarly, when employees in the workplace are engaged, organisations excel and produce more profits.

Most of us experience a wonderful feeling when someone recognises us for a meaningful contribution we have made or for special qualities we possess. This is possible when we genuinely appreciate the goodness in others. From an organisational perspective, acknowledgements can make the difference between retaining and losing employees.

If you are losing good employees, look to their immediate boss. Instead of appreciation, some bosses humiliate employees, which becomes intolerable and leads them to seek better jobs. The lack of camaraderie, human interaction, compassion, and meaningful work all take a toll. To get from where we are to where we want to be, we need the support of others.

No one can whistle a symphony. It takes a whole orchestra to do it. Mahatma Gandhi said that we are neither dependent nor independent but interdependent, and together we form an organic whole. If we have self-knowledge, we do not need external validation, but since most of us lack self-knowledge, we need acknowledgement, appreciation, and praise—from children to senior citizens. More than 90% of people are motivated to do great work when they are appreciated.

It takes little time to appreciate, costs nothing, and could impact the recipient for a lifetime. About nine out of ten employees are in search of new jobs because they are emotionally disconnected from their workplace and feel undervalued due to a lack of appreciation. We all know that the world would be a better place with more kindness and expressions of appreciation. He who appreciates another enriches himself far more than the one he praises.

To praise is an investment in one's own happiness. George Mathew Adams said, "The poorest human being has something to give that the richest could not buy." However, it is our innate nature to take people for granted and fail to appreciate their contributions to our progress or well-being. We must learn to praise others. Without our appreciation, even the best people cannot shine. It takes very little time to make eye contact, smile, engage, or ask how someone is doing.

I was sitting on a flight when a woman hurriedly took the seat next to me. She called the taxicab agency that had dropped her off at the airport to convey her deep appreciation for getting her there on time despite heavy traffic. The driver had reassured her throughout the journey that they would arrive on time, reducing her stress. Not only did she thank the driver in person, but she also wanted the company to hear the compliment.

Author Harvey Tordoff points out the interdependency of all life forms. He says, "The point is, we are not outside; we are the components that make up the whole. By inflicting pain and suffering on others, we are inflicting it on the whole, of which we are a part. Much of today's suffering stems from the way those with power exploit the vulnerable. We cannot prevent all civil wars and acts of terrorism and tyranny, but by changing our behaviour, we can create a fairer world with better healthcare, less hunger, more education, and less exploitation."

As individuals, by changing ourselves and through kind thoughts and compassionate actions, we can be the change agents the world needs. At our own individual levels, we must all work towards unity and harmony. We should appreciate every improvement.

104. The Healing Power of Touch

The five senses that provide the foundation for our experience of reality are hearing, tasting, seeing, smelling, and touching.

When we were in the mother's womb, we were in touch with the mother's body for as long as we were there. When we came out, the "touch contact" was lost. Keeping the infant close to your body whenever it cries brings relief to the child, and many times it stops crying.

Touch is a vital aspect of human connection and plays a significant role in building—

Emotional Intimacy: Touch releases oxytocin, the "love hormone," which deepens emotional intimacy and bonding.

Physical Comfort: Touch provides physical comfort, reassurance, and relaxation, reducing stress and anxiety.

Nonverbal Communication: Touch conveys emotions, empathy, and understanding without words.

Trust and Vulnerability: Touch requires trust and vulnerability, fostering a sense of safety and security.

Sensory Experience: Touch engages multiple senses, creating a rich and multisensory experience.

Attachment and Affection: Touch communicates affection, attachment, and love, strengthening relationship bonds.

Conflict Resolution: Touch can diffuse tension and facilitate conflict resolution.

Intimacy and Romance: Touch is essential for physical intimacy and romance, keeping the spark alive.

Empathy and Compassion: Touch shows empathy and compassion, supporting each other through life's challenges.

Overall Well-being: Touch has numerous physical and mental health benefits, contributing to overall well-being.

Holding your hands with your friend or spouse or relatives when they are going through tough times, looking into their eyes and saying, "I am there for you" can be a great reassurance. It helps them in the healing and enables them to come out of the difficulty very soon.

The inventor of "Touch phones" realised that touch is an emotion and that's how the "Touch phones" were born! One could see people always caressing their mobile since that is the one which is always available! People are so lonely and always bored. They always need some kind of stimuli from the world outside. When there isn't much to see, hear, taste, or smell, they have something to "touch!" However, the mobile phones are only second best but a "Touch" nevertheless!

105. Bananas and Bureaucracy

About three decades ago, the concept of having vice presidents in corporate organisations emerged. In one prominent industry, nearly every employee was given the title of vice president. There were vice presidents for the human resources department, marketing, production, operations, and even sanitation, gardening, maintenance, MIS, logistics, and many more. This was before mobile phones became common in 1995.

One day, someone called this unique corporate enterprise, and the conversation went like this:

Caller: Good morning, is this ACDRG company?

Receptionist: Yes, sir. How can I help you today?

Caller: I want to speak with Mr. John. Can you please connect me to him?

Receptionist: Certainly, sir. May I know which department?

Caller: I don't know the department, but I know his designation. He said he is a vice president.

Receptionist: Sir, there are several people named John, and they are all vice presidents. I need to know the department to help you.

Caller: Angrily, my friend John works in the banana distribution department.

The receptionist checked the EPABX extension number and replied, "Sir, is it ripe bananas or unripe bananas?"

Frustrated, the caller hung up the phone and decided never to speak to his friend John again, vowing not to reconnect even if they met in person since John didn't specify his designation!

106. The Stranger Who Became Part of the Family

A few years after I was born, my dad met a stranger who was new to our city. From the beginning, dad was fascinated with this enchanting newcomer and soon invited him to live with our family. The stranger was quickly accepted and became a constant presence in our lives.

As I grew up, I never questioned his place in our family. In my young mind, he held a special niche. My parents were complementary instructors: Mom taught me right from wrong, and dad taught me to obey. But the stranger? He was our storyteller. He captivated us for hours with tales of adventure, mystery, and comedy.

Whenever I wanted to know about politics, history, or science, he always had the answers. He seemed to know everything about the past, understood the present, and even predicted the future. He made me laugh and cry. The stranger never stopped talking, but dad didn't seem to mind.

Sometimes, mom would quietly leave while the rest of us shushed each other to listen to him, retreating to the kitchen for some peace and quiet. (I wonder now if she ever prayed for the stranger to leave.)

Dad ruled our household with firm moral convictions, but the stranger never felt obliged to honour them. Profanity, for example, was not allowed in our home—from us, our friends, or any visitors. Yet our long-time visitor got away with using four-letter words that burned my ears, made dad squirm, and caused mom to blush. Dad didn't permit the liberal use of alcohol, but the stranger encouraged us to try it regularly. He made cigarettes look cool, cigars manly, and pipes distinguished. His comments were sometimes blatant, sometimes suggestive, and generally embarrassing.

I now realise that my early concepts about relationships were heavily influenced by the stranger. Time after time, he opposed my parents' values, yet he was seldom rebuked and never asked to leave.

More than forty years have passed since the stranger moved in with our family. He has blended right in and is not nearly as fascinating as he once was. Still, if you walked into my parents' home today, you would find him sitting in his corner, waiting for someone to listen to him and watch him draw his pictures.

His name?

We just call him TV.

He has a wife now – we call her "Computer." Their first child is Cell Phone. Their second child is Video Games. And they have a wonderful grandchild: she's a genius! She is fondly called WhatsApp. She is nearly more popular than her mom. Her older cousin is Facebook, and her new baby cousins are Snapchat and Instagram.

This stranger and his family seem to have taken up permanent residence in our home, and we seem powerless to check their excesses.

107. Keep Your Problems to Yourself

A second standard boy writes a letter. It reads:

Dear Math,

I don't want to solve your problems; I have enough of my own!

108. Intimate Affairs

Son: Dad, there's a small get-together at school tomorrow at 4 p.m.

Dad: How small is the get-together?

Son: Just the three of us. You, me, and the principal.

109. A Ministerial Dilemma

An MLA called the Chief Minister's residence early in the morning. After several attempts, he finally reached the Chief Minister's assistant. The MLA said, "I need to speak to the Chief Minister immediately. It's an emergency."

Reluctantly, the assistant handed the phone to the Chief Minister. The Chief Minister, irritated by the disturbance, asked, "What made you call at such an ungodly hour?"

The MLA replied, "Sir, one of your ministers has just died, and I want to take his place."

The Chief Minister responded, "I have no objection to you taking the minister's place, but you should check if the crematorium staff would agree." With that, he hung up.

110. A Lifesaving Lesson in Effective Communication

In an emergency, communicate only in English. Avoid saying prayers in another language to prevent potential translation issues.

An Indian man living in the U.S. experienced a heart attack on the road and was taken by ambulance. Being devout, he kept repeating, "Hari Om, Hari Om, Hari Om." When the ambulance arrived at his home, his wife came out and yelled at the paramedics, "Why didn't you take him straight to the hospital?" They responded, "He kept saying, 'Hurry home! Hurry home! Hurry home!'"

111. In the Depths of Winter

A tiny little bird living in North America, like most birds that fly south during winter, this little bird missed the timing. It was winter, and it was freezing cold. The little bird's feathers got frozen and so it could not fly, despite its efforts. It fell down and was shivering in the cold. Just then, a cow was passing by. It dropped a big volume of dung on the bird.

The warmth of the dung thawed the bird, and out of sheer joy, it started to make chirping noises. Just then, a cat was passing by; it stopped to make an inquiry as to where the sound was coming from. It was coming from inside the dung. The cat cleared the dung, caught the bird, and ate it.

There are a few morals that we can learn from this story:

- One needs to be aware of the seasonal changes and be in touch with the flock.

- Not everyone who drops dung on you is your enemy.

- Not everyone who takes you out of shit is your friend.

- When you are in deep shit, you ought to keep your mouth shut!

112. Quills and Thrills

Q: How do porcupines fight with one another?

A: Very carefully!

113. The Spiritual Power of Laughter

Laughter resonates deeply with spirituality, sometimes equalling the effects of meditation. This idea is referred to as hasya yoga. While meditation typically involves concentrating on a single point, laughter transcends that focus, dissolving it entirely, and you are lost in the whole.

In this way, laughter creates a thought-free state. As a result, hasya yoga is regarded as a more profound experience than meditation, according to our elders. One could embrace this viewpoint with an open heart. We need to keep in mind that laughter is harmoniously aligned with spirituality, not opposed to it!

One should also remember that laughter should not be directed against anyone; it should celebrate life and living.

114. Meditation:
A Journey to Mastering the Mind, Not Controlling It

Most of us are quite familiar with the art of meditation and have accumulated valuable experience in it. It's been observed that when the mind is at ease, everything else tends to fall into place. This inner peace and happiness are vital for every individual. Historically, around 400 to 500 years ago, people already faced significant tension. Today, however, this tension has increased by about 40%, highlighting a substantial change over time.

Imagine that six hundred years ago, there was a 1 kg weight resting on the head; today, that weight has multiplied to 40 kg! This illustrates the exponential rise in tension over the centuries. This increase in stress can be linked to new discoveries and advancements in science, which, while providing convenience, also contribute to our stress. For example, it was only with the advent of electricity that we began to worry about power outages; before that, the concept didn't even exist.

Such innovations offer convenience but also heighten mental activity, leading to more discoveries and, consequently, greater stress. Therefore, finding a way to maintain peace of mind is essential—a form of penance we all require. Esteemed teachers have long emphasised the importance of keeping our minds calm. Many people try to control their minds, but this effort often leads to greater restlessness. Instead, understanding the mind is the key to mastery.

The goal should be to comprehend our minds rather than try to control them. Those who grasp this concept can truly appreciate its significance. Consider the story of a man who ventured into a forest to find control over his mind, believing he would be free from distractions there. He selected a quiet spot beneath a tree, away from the chaos, to concentrate. However, each morning at 8 am, a young woman would pass by on her way to dance school, disrupting his focus.

The following day, he covered his eyes with a cloth, thinking it would eliminate the distraction. Yet, he still heard her footsteps and attempted to block his ears. Then, the scent of the flowers she wore distracted him, leading him to block his sense of smell. Despite his efforts, at exactly 8 am the next day, he found his mind wandering again, preoccupied with whether she had passed by. He was left wondering which sense to obstruct next!

This experience illustrates the essence of spirituality, which centres on understanding the mind, not controlling it. Striving to control the mind often leads to further distractions. Instead, by seeking to understand it, you can genuinely gain control. Therefore, the focus should be on understanding the mind rather than trying to control it.

Meditation doesn't control our mind, but rather helps us become more aware of our thoughts, emotions, and behaviours. Regular meditation practice can:

- Calm your mind and reduce stress.

- Increase focus and concentration.

- Enhance self-awareness and introspection.

- Improve emotional regulation.

Meditation teaches you to observe your thoughts without judgement, allowing one to:

- Recognise patterns and habits

- Make conscious choices

- Cultivate a sense of inner peace and clarity.

Remember, meditation is a tool to harmonise your mind, not control it. It's a journey of self-discovery and growth!

115. The Cost of Anger

One day at Mumbai International Airport, a passenger bound for Japan was struggling with an excessive amount of luggage. When it was time to board, he grew furious and nearly lashed out at the airline staff. His face was twisted with rage, and his temper was palpable. Yet, the staff member remained unfazed, calmly repeating, "Okay, sir," with a polite smile. Despite the passenger's escalating anger, the employee stayed composed and professional.

The manager, quietly observing from nearby, kept his own calm demeanour as the situation unfolded. As the passengers' frustration intensified, the airline staff continued to smile and handle the encounter gracefully.

Curious, the manager asked, "How are you able to respond to such rude behaviour with a polite smile and such grace?"

The staff member grinned and replied, "Simple, sir. The passenger is headed to Japan, but his luggage is going to America!"

Anger is a luxury no one can afford. The cost is always too high.

"It's natural for everyone to feel angry at times, but what benefit is there in letting anger take control? We must learn to manage our emotions instead of letting them manage us."

116. A Birthday Surprise from IIT Madras

We live on the seventh-floor of an apartment complex, located about 4 km from IIT Madras. The area between us and IIT Madras is lush with vegetation, separated by a river.

One morning around 11 am, two air conditioning mechanics were working on our AC unit in one of the bedrooms. They had left their toolbox near the dining area, and one technician went to retrieve a cutting plier. To his surprise, he saw a large adult monkey sitting on the dining table, enjoying the birthday cake we had bought for my son's celebration.

The mechanic was shocked, and when he tried to scare the monkey away, it responded by scowling and baring its teeth. Frightened, the mechanic ran toward the main door, which was fully open. My wife, who was in the kitchen, was petrified at the sight of the grown-up monkey sitting at the table, eating the cake.

When the mechanic returned with three more people, the monkey quickly jumped off the table and escaped through the main door with a large piece of cake in its mouth.

Later that week, during our executive committee meeting, I recounted the incident excitedly as the president of the committee before moving on to the agenda points, emphasising how the monkey must have come from IIT Madras. I joked that only IIT monkeys ventured so far and wide! I repeated this a couple of times, only to notice an EC member glaring at me.

I soon realised the reason for his disapproving look: he was an alumnus of IIT Madras, having graduated several decades ago. Recognising my mistake, I quickly shifted the focus back to the agenda for the meeting.

117. Heightened Awareness

At the entrance of Heathrow Airport, a signboard was found stating, "Dogs not allowed beyond this point." Interestingly, the signboard was mounted at a height of about 2 feet, perfect for dogs to see and take note of!

118. Nearest Correct Answer

In a bank interview many years ago, a candidate was asked a straightforward question: "What is 3 multiplied by 13?" Confidently, he responded, "38." The interviewer replied, "We'll get back to you." As the candidate left the room, he realised his grave mistake; in his haste, he had blurted out 38, though he knew the answer was 39. He felt sure he had lost the job.

To his surprise, he received an appointment letter from the bank and joined the team. Curious to know if the interviewer had misheard his answer or believed it was correct, he waited until his probation period ended. Once confirmed in his position, he approached the interviewer and asked, "Sir, you asked me what is the value when three is multiplied by 13? I replied 38, and I still don't understand how I got the job. Did you not hear my wrong answer, or did no one provide the correct answer?"

The interviewer responded, "Please sit; I'll explain what happened that day. During the interview, we had fifty-six candidates, including you. I asked all of them the same question, 'What is three multiplied by 13?' Your answer was the closest, which is why we offered you the job!"

This story illustrates the importance of accuracy, particularly in fields like science. For instance, a calculation error by a scientist could cause a satellite meant for Mars to land on another planet. However, in life, what matters is the closest correct answer, not necessarily a perfect one. Striving for perfection in all aspects can lead to stress. To live a stress-free life, it's not essential to be perfect in every aspect.

119. One Common Habit of Billionaires

Shiv Khera, a renowned motivational speaker, is best known for his bestselling book *You Can Win*. In an interview, he was asked, "What do billionaires have in common?"

He responded, "Around 85% of billionaires started from scratch, while the rest joined already established enterprises." He further noted, "One key insight from interviewing them is that they all embraced reading—not fiction, but self-help books. They believe that even a single idea from such books can multiply their revenue."

How true! Just one sentence, one inspiring thought, or one idea from a book can truly transform our lives for the better.

120. The Art of Survival!

At a party full of celebrities, a grey-haired veteran hobbled to the stage, leaned on his cane, and took a seat.

The host asked, "Do you still visit the doctor often?"

The veteran replied, "Yes, often."

The host continued, "Why?"

The veteran quipped, "Because patients must visit doctors often! Only then can doctors survive!"

The audience erupted into warm applause, cheering for the veteran's optimistic and witty response.

The host then asked, "Do you often ask the hospital pharmacist about how to take your medicine?"

The veteran answered, "Yes, I often ask the pharmacist how to take my medicine! Because the pharmacist needs to make a living, too!"

Another round of applause echoed through the room.

The host then inquired, "Do you take your medicine often?"

The veteran responded, "No! I often throw away the medicine because I want to survive, too!"

The audience roared with laughter.

The host concluded, "Thank you for accepting my interview!"

The veteran replied, "You're welcome! I know you have to survive, too!"

The audience burst into laughter, applause, and cheers that went on for a long time.

The host asked another question, "Do you still chat in the group often?"

The veteran replied, "Yes, I also want to survive in the group! If I don't show up and don't chat, everyone will think I'm dead, and the group admin will delete me!"

121. The Barber's Paradox

A man went to a barbershop for a haircut and beard trim. As the barber started working, he began a friendly conversation, covering a variety of topics. Eventually, the conversation turned to the topic of God.

The barber expressed his disbelief, saying, "I don't believe that God exists."

"Why do you say that?" the customer inquired.

"Well, just look around," the barber responded. "If God existed, would there be so many sick people? Would there be abandoned children? If there were a loving God, there wouldn't be so much suffering and pain."

The customer paused to think but chose not to argue. After the barber finished his job, the customer left the shop. Outside, he noticed a man with long, stringy, dirty hair and an untrimmed beard, looking unkempt.

The customer returned to the barbershop and said, "You know what? Barbers don't exist."

The barber, surprised, asked, "How can you say that? I'm here, and I just worked on you!"

"No," the customer replied. "Barbers don't exist because if they did, people like that man outside wouldn't have long, dirty hair and untrimmed beards."

The barber explained, "Barbers do exist. The problem is, people don't come to me."

"Exactly!" the customer affirmed. "That's the point! God, too, does exist. The problem is, people don't go to Him or seek Him out. That's why there's so much pain and suffering in the world."

122. The Roar of Vanity

Early one morning, a lion awoke in a boisterous mood. He went out, found a small monkey, and roared, "Who is the mightiest of all the jungle animals?"

The frightened monkey replied, "You are, mighty lion!"

Next, the lion encountered a deer and thundered, "Who is the mightiest of all the jungle animals?"

The terrified deer stuttered, "Oh great lion, you are without a doubt the mightiest animal in the jungle!"

Feeling unstoppable, the lion swaggered over to an elephant and roared, "Who is the mightiest of all the jungle animals?"

The elephant picked up the lion with its trunk, slammed it against a tree, stomped on it, and then walked away.

The bruised lion called out after the elephant, "You freak, just because you don't know the answer doesn't mean you have to get so upset."

123. Friendship Cures Fear

A man visited his family doctor because he was experiencing palpitations. The doctor conducted a thorough examination, checking his blood pressure, pulse, and ECG. With a reassuring smile, the doctor told him, "You are perfectly alright, but you need to let go of your fear. Remember, FEAR stands for 'False Evidence Appearing Real.' Spend time with your classmates and old friends; they're the best remedy for your worries and ailments.

I won't prescribe any medication since your vitals are in great shape. Staying connected with your classmates and friends is essential because they are the healers who can comfort you with their sweet and sometimes teasing words. These friends don't let you feel your age; they keep you young and are always there to walk beside you. They help you live in the present, allowing you to forget your anxieties and worries.

While children might ask about your will, relatives might inquire about your bill, and doctors might suggest a pill, only your classmates and old friends will remind you to 'JUST Chill!'

124. Application for the Technical Manager Position

Dear Hiring Manager,

I am writing to express my interest in the Technical Manager position at your company. I understand that this role has recently become available due to the unfortunate passing of the previous manager, a loss that I know has been deeply felt within your organisation.

I have applied for several positions in your company over the past several years, often encountering replies that no vacancies were available. However, with this position now open, I am eager to seize the opportunity to contribute my skills and experience to your team. My attendance at the funeral was not only to pay my respects but also to confirm my readiness to fill this crucial role.

Please find attached my resume, which details my qualifications and experience, along with the death certificate of the deceased!

Thank you for considering my application. I look forward to the possibility of contributing to your company's success.

Sincerely,

125. Power Play

Q: Who is stronger: Batman, Spider-Man, Superman, Iron Man, or the lineman?

A: The lineman is by far the strongest because his power is quite literally in his hands!

126. Who is a Guru, and Why Do We Need One?

A "Guru" is a Sanskrit term where "Gu" translates to darkness, and "Ru" translates to remover. Therefore, a Guru is one who removes darkness. This metaphorical darkness represents ignorance, confusion, or lack of direction in life.

The Importance of a Guide

Imagine navigating through a busy road network with multiple exits and entry points. Without a guiding voice, such as that of a GPS system, reaching your destination can be challenging. Similarly, in the complex maze of life, we often find ourselves lost, unsure of which path to take. A Guru serves as this essential guide, helping us navigate through the confusion and uncertainty.

Seeing the Bigger Picture:

While we see only the walls of the maze around us, a Guru has a broader perspective, much like viewing the maze from above. This aerial view allows the Guru to guide us towards the exit, helping us make decisions that we might otherwise be unable to see on our own.

In essence, just as a GPS system helps us find our way in the physical world, a Guru assists us in finding our spiritual or personal path. Thus, we can think of the term "GPS" as "Guru's Positioning System," guiding us towards enlightenment and clarity.

127. Going Offline

Stepping "offline" for a few minutes can help anchor us in the present moment, fostering a state of full awareness and focus on the here and now. This "present-minute awareness" involves being fully conscious of what's happening right now, free from distractions about the past or future. This practice is closely linked to mindfulness, where we maintain continuous awareness of our thoughts, feelings, bodily sensations, and surroundings.

Q: Why did the meditation teacher break up with their partner?

A: Because they couldn't stop living in the past and future—there was just no present connection!

Practising present-minute awareness can reduce stress, sharpen mental clarity, and improve overall well-being by encouraging us to fully engage with our current experiences. It's about truly living in the now and embracing life as it happens.

When you go "offline," your focus naturally shifts to immediate aspects of life—like your meals, work, family, weekends, and vacations. This is one's "circle of influence" where one can have their 'say' and get it done. This could give one a feeling of fulfilment.

On the other hand, when you're "online," your attention often broadens to encompass larger issues, such as religion, politics, society, culture, environmental conservation, privatisation, healthcare, global warming, philosophy; more importantly things that are not personally relevant like the vast world of social media. This is called the "circle of concern" where you can have a say but the world will have its own way!

128. The Mystery of Mysore Throat

The manager received a leave letter from Vishwanath Shetty, explaining that he had "Madras eye," a contagious condition, and would be taking time off. Recognising the contagious nature of the illness, the manager agreed it was best for Vishwanath to stay home.

A few weeks later, Vishwanath sent another leave letter, this time stating he couldn't come to work due to "Mysore throat." The manager was puzzled, as he'd never heard of "Mysore throat" before. Curious, he googled the term, but his research didn't yield any clear results. Unsure, he decided not to question it, thinking there might indeed be something called "Mysore throat"—especially since he himself was from Mysore and didn't want to appear uninformed.

The next day, when Vishwanath returned to the office, the manager asked with concern, "Vishwanath, how is your Mysore throat?" Vishwanath looked confused and replied, "I just had a sore throat, that's why I didn't come to work yesterday. I don't have anything called 'Mysore throat!"

The manager then showed him the email from the previous day, where it clearly read "Mysore throat." Vishwanath laughed and said, "Oh, I'm sorry, sir! That was a typo. It was supposed to say 'My sore throat!'"

129. The Breath of Change

One day, a thief approached the Buddha and said, "I want to learn meditation, but I'm a thief and can't stop stealing. What should I do?"

The Buddha calmly replied, "Why worry about giving up stealing? Meditation has nothing to do with your actions."

Surprised and puzzled, the thief looked at the Buddha, who continued, "Go ahead and do whatever you wish, but never stop observing your breath. In every situation, keep watching your breath."

The thief, thinking this was simple, said, "That sounds easy enough."

The next day, the thief returned to the Buddha, looking exhausted and frustrated. He said, "You tricked me."

The Buddha asked, "What happened?"

The thief replied, "I tried to steal yesterday, but as I observed my breath, I couldn't do it properly. I ended up not stealing at all. Now what should I do?"

The Buddha explained, "When you observe your breath, you become fully alert and aware. In that state, it's impossible to commit any wrong. This is the meditation I'm teaching you."

According to history, the Buddha himself attained enlightenment through this practice. Try this meditation technique to enhance your awareness.

130. The Irony of Happiness

We dream of making lots of money, yet our happiest memories are from times when we only had a few dollars in our pocket.

We desire to wear luxury brands, but we feel most at ease in our favourite jeans.

We aspire to dine at five-star hotels with the elite, but nothing beats the joy of sharing a roadside tea with friends.

We long to own luxury cars and go on long drives, but the most heartfelt conversations happen while walking down a quiet street.

We fill our 64GB iPods with countless songs, yet sometimes, it's a random tune on the radio that truly makes us smile.

Life is indeed simple, but we complicate it by chasing things that don't bring true happiness.

Happiness is in the small things.

Success is in the big things.

Meditation is in nothing and

God is in everything.

The recipe for being happy is: 1) Love people and use things; not the other way around! 2) Celebrate life. 3) Appreciate the costless luxuries and relish the small moments. 4) Keep smiling knowing that this too shall pass!

131. Bill Collectors from Beyond

"Cancel Your Credit Card Before You Die: A Hilarious Story!'

In January 2016, a lady passed away. However, her bank continued to bill her for annual service charges on her credit card in February and March of 2016, tacking on late fees and interest as well.

When she passed, her balance was Rs 0.00, but by March, it had grown to around Rs 6000.

A concerned family member decided to call the bank. Here's how the conversation went:

Family Member: "I'm calling to inform you that she passed away in January 2016."

Bank: "The account was never closed, so the late fees and charges still apply."

Family Member: "Perhaps you should transfer this to your collections department?"

Bank: "It's already been handed over since it's two months overdue."

Family Member: "And what will they do when they discover she's deceased?"

Bank: "We might report it to the fraud department or the credit bureau – or maybe both!"

Family Member: "Do you think God will be angry with her?"

Bank: "Excuse me?"

Family Member: "Did you catch the part about her being dead?"

Bank: "Sir, you'll need to speak with my supervisor."

The supervisor comes on the line.

Family Member: "I'm calling to let you know that she passed away in January 2016, with a Rs 0 balance on her credit card."

Bank: "The account wasn't closed, so late fees and charges still apply."

Family Member: "Are you trying to collect from her estate?"

Bank: (Stammering) "Are you her lawyer?"

Family Member: "No, I'm her grandnephew."

Bank: "Could you fax us a death certificate?"

Family Member: "Sure." (Fax number provided)

After receiving the fax:

Bank: "Our system isn't set up for death. I'm not sure what else I can do."

Family Member: "Well, if you figure it out, great! If not, you can keep billing her. She won't mind."

Bank: "The late fees and charges will still apply."

(What is wrong with these people?)

Family Member: "Would you like her new billing address?"

Bank: "That might help..."

Family Member: "Quibble Island Cemetery, Grave no. 1528, Foreshore Estate, Chennai."

Bank: "Sir, that's a cemetery!"

Family Member: "And what do you do with dead people on your planet?"

132. Bridal Wit and Humour

The newlywed husband's friends invited the couple for a get-together, followed by cocktails and dinner. As is typical when friends gather, light-hearted banter filled the room. Eventually, the conversation turned more direct, with questions for the new bride about her husband and in-laws.

One friend asked, "It's been a month since your wedding. Do you like your husband?"

The bride blushed and replied, "Oh yes!" Thanks for asking, and she turned and winked at her husband.

Another friend then asked, "And what about the in-laws? Do you like them?"

With a playful smile, the bride responded, "Oh yes, I love my husband's in-laws!"

All the friends took a second to understand the answer and burst into laughter, appreciating her quick wit and humour.

133. Lessons Beyond the Classroom

In a class test, one of the questions was, "Write a brief paragraph about Raja Ram Mohan Roy." One of the back benchers had written, "All the four were good friends!"

The teacher called the boy and told him, "Your answer is not correct?"

The boy retorted, "Why, sir, don't you want all four to be happy?"

The front benchers gave the loudest jeer and mockingly looked at the last bencher.

The teacher told the class, "The answer is wrong, but from my experience, let me tell you that most of the backbenchers start their own entrepreneurial firm and employ many people." He added that most of the front benchers are too good at giving exams, filling out application forms, doing well in competitive exams, excelling in interviews, and landing lucrative jobs.

The point I am trying to make is that, "not all who score well in exams make it good in life and not all who do badly in exams don't make it good in life."

Academics are different. Life is different!

The class sat in pin-drop silence deliberating on a profound statement, until the bell rang!

134. Cheers to Choices

Two friends who hadn't seen each other in a while met at a restaurant. One was a teetotaller, while the other enjoyed his drinks. They caught up on various topics like food, the cost of living, work, vacations, and stress. The drinking friend was on his fourth round, while the teetotaller sipped slowly on a fruit punch. Their conversation went something like this:

Teetotaller: "How long have you been drinking?"

Friend (who drinks): "Maybe 25 years or more."

Teetotaller: "Let's assume you buy three bottles of beer every day, spending about Rs 12,000 each month. Over a year, that adds up to around Rs 144,000. Does that sound right?"

Friend: (after thinking for a moment) "Roughly, yes."

Teetotaller: "Now, if you'd saved and invested that money wisely, with compound interest at 7.5% annually, in about 25 years you could have accumulated around Rs 1 crore—enough to buy a Mercedes Benz with a fancy number plate."

Friend: (grinning) "You're right. So, you're saying that if I had saved Rs 12,000 per month for 25 years, compounded annually, I'd have about Rs 1 crore by now."

Teetotaller: (confidently, thinking he's made his point) "Exactly!"

Friend: (now a bit more serious) "So, where's your Mercedes Benz?"

135. Heroic Rescue at Sea

A luxury cruise ship was sailing through the Pacific Ocean when the captain made an announcement over the public address system. He informed the passengers that they were passing over the deepest point in the ocean, the Mariana Trench, which plunges to a depth of 36,037 feet. He added that even Mount Everest, with its elevation of 29,024 feet, could be submerged in the trench.

Excited by the news, many passengers began taking selfies, capturing the moment. Among them, a girl leaned too far backwards, lost her balance, and fell overboard from the deck where others were admiring the majestic view.

Chaos ensued as panic spread among the passengers. While lifeguards scrambled to launch lifeboats and shouts filled the air, no one dared to jump in. Then, suddenly, an elderly man, over eighty years old, dove into the ocean and managed to rescue the young woman, bringing her safely into a lifeboat. Once back on board, paramedics quickly attended to her, and she soon recovered.

That evening, the captain announced a party to honour the elderly man who had risked his life to save the young woman. He presented the man with a $10,000 cash reward and invited him to share a few words about his brave deed.

The old man accepted the money, thanked the captain, and said, "You've made me a hero today, and that's fine. But all I really want to know is— who was the rascal that pushed me into the sea?"

136. A Cultural Drive from Chennai

A Chinese man landed at Chennai airport; the taxi arranged by a star hotel in Mahabalipuram picked him up to be dropped off at Mahabalipuram.

On his way, upon seeing a bus after Guindy, he told the taxi driver that in Chennai buses run very slowly. In China, buses run very fast.

After some time, he came to Tiruvanmiyur signal, said the signal was very slow! In China, the signal turns very fast.

They tried to pass a truck. The Chinese man said, "This truck is very slow! In China, we have a 12-lane highway, and trucks go at a minimum of 120 km/h!"

Then they came to Neelankarai signal. The signal was not working, and a traffic policeman was on duty. The Chinese man said, "This policeman is lethargic. Look how slow he is moving and showing signals! In China, our policemen are like tigers; they move very fast!"

Tamilians, being very polite and humble, the taxi driver kept quiet and kept nodding throughout the journey.

When they reached the hotel, the Chinese man asked the driver, "What is the meter reading?"

The taxi driver replied, "It is Rs. 9500."

The Chinese man was shell-shocked. He shouted, "Are you kidding? In your country, buses run slow, trucks are slow, signals are slow, and cops too... everything is slow. How come the meter alone runs fast?"

Taxi driver: Sir, "The meter is made in China!"

137. The First Step to Safe Driving

This occurred at a regional transport office, where the inspector in charge of certifying new drivers posed this question:

Q: Which part of the car's interior/exterior moves first, long before anything else?

Many people guessed, saying "the number plate, the bumper, the fog lights, the headlights, the spoilers," but none of them passed the oral test. The licence issuing officer then gathered everyone and confessed, "Even I failed this test long ago because I didn't know the correct answer."

The correct answer is: "our vision!"

138. A Lesson Beyond Degrees

The man asked the boy, "Which class are you in?"

"Second Standard. And you?" the boy replied.

"I've finished my studies," the man said.

"Did you study up to any class?" the boy inquired.

"Ph.D.," the man said.

"Is that higher than the second standard?" The man smiled.

The boy's father intervened, "Hey, you shouldn't ask like that."

"It's alright. No harm," the man assured him.

The bus travelling from Chennai to Madurai had stopped at a roadside hotel for a break. It was two in the morning, yet the place was bustling with passengers enjoying dishes like masala dosa, paratha, and chapati.

"In which field did you get your Ph.D.?" asked the boy's father.

"Automobile engineering," the man replied.

"What's an automobile engine?" the boy asked curiously.

"Hmm, you wouldn't understand," the father interjected.

"No, no, no... That's where we go wrong. Never discourage children when they ask questions," the man with the Ph.D. in automobile engineering insisted.

"We're on a bus, which is an automobile. Do you know how it works?" he asked the boy.

"Mmmm," the boy mumbled.

"The class I studied covers all that,"

"Tell me how it works?"

The man sat the boy on his lap and began explaining. He talked about motorcycles, diesel engines, two-stroke and four-stroke engines, spark ignition, compression ignition, speed, and torque. The boy listened intently, hanging on every word.

Finally, the man asked, "Do you understand everything about the bus now?"

The boy nodded with a smile.

After everyone had finished eating, they boarded the bus again. When the driver tried to start the engine, it wouldn't start. The driver and conductor were at a loss.

"If we call someone from the Villupuram depot, it'll take three hours," one said.

"What should we do now?" the other asked.

"Maybe call a local mechanic?"

"It's already 2:15."

The boy went to the conductor and suggested, "This uncle knows everything about the bus."

The conductor was taken aback. "Sir, are you a mechanic?"

"No, I have a doctorate, a Ph.D. in Automobile Engineering," the man replied.

"Oh, Doctor... My apologies," the conductor said, disappointed.

The boy's father scolded him, "Ramesh, don't trouble him."

Meanwhile, the driver had fetched a scruffy young man who had been sleeping at the door of a nearby mechanic shop. The mechanic took a quick look under the hood, fiddled with a small valve, and then said, "Try starting it now."

The bus roared to life.

"Driver! Don't turn off the engine until it's properly fixed," the mechanic advised, accepting the fifty rupees the driver handed him with a smile.

The boy was amazed. He approached the mechanic and asked, "Did you also do a Ph.D.?"

"No," the mechanic replied, puzzled. What is a Ph.D.?"

"Do you know about petrol engines and diesel engines?"

"I only know about pedal bicycles and a little about some repairs,"

"Do you understand the relationship between speed and torque?"

"No, I don't have any relatives!"

"Did you study buses in college?"

"I never went to school," the mechanic admitted.

The boy thought for a moment and then smiled, saying to himself, "I understand now."

He returned to his seat, but the man with the Ph.D. seemed a bit bothered.

"What did you understand?" the man asked the boy.

"People who study get paid a lot. But the uneducated know what the educated don't. But they don't get paid as much. The salary is for studies, not for knowing things experientially," the boy told the PhD. He then thought to himself, "When I grow up, I want to understand the practical as well as the theory behind it."

139. Unearthing Purpose in Existence

One apprentice had joined a Buddhist monastery and at the end of 6 months declared in front of fellow apprentices and their teacher, "My observation over the last 6 months is that there is vastness in space and darkness inside; there is no meaning to life." "Everything is meaningless. Our life is meaningless; the whole existence is meaningless." In fact, he challenged the teacher that this whole world lacks meaning and welcomed him to prove otherwise if he thought so!"

The teacher said, "Everything has a meaning and its design is such that we need to 'create' our own meaning."

The student retorted, "Even the design of existence is meaningless."

The teacher said, "Everything has a meaning; the design is such that we need to find our own meaning." He explained: Thirty spokes share the wheel's hub; it is the centre hole that makes it useful. Shape clay into a vessel; it is the space within that makes it useful. Cut doors and windows for a room; it is the holes/space inside the room which make it useful. Therefore, Function and Profit come from what is there; Usefulness comes from what is not there.

The teacher continued, "Existence is a vast canvas which invites your Creative Contribution for the universe's evolution. The apprentice as well as other apprentices were overwhelmed by the clarity of the teacher's explanation which originated from Lao Tzu's teachings."

140. The Triple Filter Test

The lion in the jungle was very hungry and had set out on its hunt. It saw a young spotted deer which had just got separated from its mother. It went near the deer, but sympathy took over the lion and it did not kill the deer; instead, it took it to his cave. Wherever he went, the spotted deer accompanied him. Other animals were happy, but one wolf wasn't.

It thought of scheming the lion and separating the deer from its caretaker. It went to the cave and asked the lion if he could come in. The lion said, "If you have a reason, step forward."

The wolf said it had a reason, and the lion welcomed the wolf. The lion asked the wolf the reason for his visit. The wolf said that he heard a lot of bad things about the deer that was under the lion's shelter, and just to update the lion about the deer.

The lion said, "Just before you say anything, please answer the three questions:

Lion: Is what you are going to say about the deer true? Did you see it?

Jackal: No, Your Majesty.

Lion: Are you going to say something good about the deer?

Jackal: No, Your Majesty.

Lion: Is what you are going to say going to be useful to everyone in the jungle?

Jackal: No, Your Majesty. (He thought to himself that what he had in his mind would be useful only to him, but he dares not say!)

Lion: I now understand the bad intention and motive behind your visit. Now, before I kill you, run away and save yourself.

The jackal ran away to safety.

This is the triple filter test conducted by Socrates: People are happy to gossip all about others, 99% of them are not true, not good for the community, nor useful to anyone. Gossip rids one of their vital energies, thereby affecting the clarity of thinking since their intellect is compromised.

141. The Power of Laughter, Praise, and Gratitude in Everyday Life

We've forgotten to laugh, to enjoy, to experience, to praise, and to feel grateful. We're all searching for happiness, but if we do all these things, happiness will come on its own.

When you laugh, people return it back to you. Let's continue that cycle of laughter.

Next time you watch a YouTube video, listen first to understand, then watch again to enjoy. Before moving on, take a moment to praise in the comment section. You might not be here to study, but learning to give praise is valuable for you. When you eat at a restaurant and if you find the food good and services great, compliment the chef and the waiter. Learn to praise people all the time when they do all the right things right.

Learn to experience life fully. Wearing a nice dress or a new pair of shoes—those are experiences. Embrace everything in life. Live life intensely with choiceless awareness and without judgement.

If one could cultivate the attitude of gratitude, everything else will fall into place. Make it a daily habit to thank all the time for all the smallest favours. Develop these qualities and stop searching for happiness—happiness will come to you naturally.

142. Braking for Success: Lessons from the Classroom

The class teacher asked the students, "Why are brakes provided in cars and other automobiles?"

Some of the students answered like 1) "To control speed; 2) to ensure the safety of people on the road and passengers in the car; 3) for emergency stopping; to maintain stability and better handling during cornering or when driving on slippery surfaces."

The teacher smiled and said, "Good attempts, but none of these are the correct answer. Can anyone think of another reason?"

One student stood up and asked, "Is it to increase speed?"

The teacher clapped and said, "Well done, that's the right answer. With brakes, we can confidently increase our speed, knowing that we can stop whenever necessary. The goal of an automobile is to take us from point A to point B quickly and safely. In today's world, speed and safety go hand in hand."

The teacher continued, "Similarly, when we face obstacles or challenges in life, they shouldn't slow us down or cause us to give up. Just like brakes allow us to speed up, challenges give us the opportunity to bring out our best, like making lemonade from lemons. The only people without problems are those who are six feet under the ground. Face your challenges head-on, and you can turn them into priceless opportunities."

143. Between Berths: An Unusual Family Conversation

Dilip was travelling on the Avantika Express from Mumbai to Indore. After a long day, he boarded the train in Mumbai, quickly climbed to his designated upper berth, and closed his eyes to rest. It was around 9 pm when the train departed, and Dilip was drifting into relaxation when his phone rang. Half-asleep, he answered.

Dilip: "Yes, who is this?"

Caller: "This is Rakesh. May I know who I'm speaking to?"

Dilip: "I'm Dilip. Rakesh? The name sounds familiar." "Where are you from?"

Caller: "I'm Rakesh from Andheri. Your name also sounds familiar."

Dilip: "Andheri East or West?"

Caller: "Andheri West."

Dilip: "I'm from Andheri West too."

Caller: "I live in Four Bungalows. What about you?"

Dilip: "I also live in Four Bungalows! What's your apartment number?"

Caller: "It's 505. And yours?"

Dilip: "Mine is 505 too."

Caller: "Where are you now?"

Dilip: "I'm on the Avantika Express in 3A. What about you?"

Caller: "I'm also on the Avantika Express, in 3A. What's your berth number?"

Dilip: "Mine is 52, upper berth. And yours?"

Caller: "Mine is 54, lower berth."

Their conversation was loud enough to disturb the passenger in the middle berth. Realising the bizarre coincidence, he couldn't help but interject, frustrated by the noise.

Middle Berth Passenger: "Aren't you aware that the person in the upper berth is from the same apartment as you? You're Rakesh, and the guy above is Dilip. Don't you know each other?"

Rakesh smiled and responded curtly, "This is our 'family time'; Dilip is my first son. This is just how we keep in touch. Why are you interfering in our family matters!"

Rakesh and Dilip continued their conversation:

Son (occupying upper berth): "Papa, are you okay down there?"

Father (occupying lower berth): "Yes, son, I'm fine. Just a bit cramped. How about you up there?"

Middle Man: (interrupting) "You know, I'm the one really feeling the strain here—stuck between your stupid, idiotic conversations!"

Son: (laughs) "Sorry, sir! We're just trying to stay connected!"

Father: (chuckles and tells the passenger in the middle berth) "I guess we're just trying to stay on the same track!"

Middle Man: (gave up and laughs) "Well, I'm just trying to stay sane!" He stuffed cotton into his ears and went to sleep.

There are innumerable ways of testing the patience of people with their non-stop chatter on trains about sweet nothings, business, or family matters, mostly after 9 pm! Patience and tolerance can be developed by travelling with these types of people!

144. The Car That Solved It All

Sanjay: Hey Jacob, "you said that you have been having a lot of problems parking your second car inside the apartment; what is the situation now?"

Jacob: "The parking problem has been resolved amicably among our friendly apartment owners. They are such nice people, you know!"

Sanjay: "How?"

Jacob: "I sold my first car!"

145. Beyond the Decorations: The True Value of Life

Aren't goals like high-paying jobs, luxurious houses, fancy cars, wealth, and power just decorations? Aren't power, positions, titles just decorations? They are psychological decorations. There are also physical ones, like having good children, a loving spouse, and so on. They are necessary to keep us going as long as we know that the life in us is far more precious than the outside decorations!

The truth is simple: the one who possesses is greater than even the greatest possession. The neck is always more valuable than the necklace. No matter how expensive the necklace is, the neck that holds it is more precious. The person is the noun, and the ornaments are merely adjectives—additional decorations. A diamond nose ring will never be more valuable than the nose it adorns. It's the nose that matters. So, don't sacrifice your neck or nose for the sake of a trivial ornament.

The goals we pursue are like ornamental adjectives; they are indeed required until a stage, but once we reach a stage in life where we have enough, we should strive to look inwards and reach "Him" because that is the end goal.

The possessor is always greater than the possession, no matter how costly or precious that possession may be. Imagine you wear a crown studded with the Kohinoor diamond and other gems. Isn't your head still greater than the crown? We're not denying the beauty or aesthetic pleasure of ornaments. If you desire the crown, by all means, strive for it. Seek it out, fight for it, and cry for it if you must. But do so without losing your peace of mind. After all, as we've noted, the head is always greater than the crown, no matter how expensive it may be.

A man was driving a car, smoking a cigarette. As he extended his hand out of the window to flick off the ash, a speeding truck passed by, severing his hand. In shock, the man cried out, "Oh my God, my Rolex watch that I just bought last month is broken!"

This illustrates the paradox of life – we often place more value on our possessions than on appreciating the gifts that life itself has given us.

146. Badge of Authority, Horns of Reality

A Narcotics department officer stopped by a farm on his way up the mountains and approached an old cattle farmer. "I need to inspect your farm," the officer said. "We have information that you're illegally growing drugs."

The farmer replied calmly, "Sure, go ahead, but please avoid that field over there," pointing to a specific area.

The officer's demeanour quickly changed. "Mister, I have the authority of the Government behind me!" he shouted. "I will go wherever I want." He reached into his back pocket, pulled out his badge, and flashed it at the farmer. "See this badge? It means I can go anywhere I choose, on any land! No questions asked, no explanations needed! Do I make myself clear?"

The farmer nodded politely, apologised, and returned to his chores.

A short while later, the farmer heard desperate screams and looked up to see the officer running for his life, being chased by the farmer's massive bull. With every step, the bull was closing in on the terrified officer, who seemed certain to be gored before he could reach safety.

The farmer dropped his tools, ran to the fence, and shouted at the top of his lungs, "Your badge! Show him your BADGE!"

147. Uncrewed and Unfazed

Imagine a scenario where 20 CEOs board a plane, only to learn that it's the first-ever flight operated entirely by pilotless technology—an uncrewed aircraft. Each CEO is then informed privately that their own company's software is in charge of the plane's autopilot system.

Upon hearing this, nineteen of the CEOs quickly disembarked, each offering a different excuse.

But one CEO stays on board, completely unruffled.

When asked why he's so confident about staying on the uncrewed flight, he responds, "If it's the same software developed by my company's IT department, this plane won't even get off the ground."

Now that is what you call confidence!

148. Dad's Tech-Savvy Response

Girl: "Dad, I'm in love with a boy who lives far away. I'm in the US, and he's in the UK. We met on a dating site, became friends on Facebook, had long chats on WhatsApp, he proposed on Skype, and we've been in a relationship for two months now through Viber. I need your blessings and good wishes, Daddy..."

Dad: "Wow! Really? Then why not get married on Twitter, celebrate on Tango, buy your kids on eBay, and send them through Gmail. And if you ever get tired of your husband... just sell him on Amazon!"

149. Prefixes and Positivity – A Study Tip from 1974

It was 1974, the night before the final exams, with the English exam looming the next day. My friend was studying English with help from his older brother. He asked, "Can you tell me a simple way to learn opposites?"

After thinking for a moment, his brother replied, "This isn't always accurate, but for you, try this method: remember these prefixes—'un,' 'non,' and 'dis.' Use them before the words you see on the exam."

He gave some examples:

If they ask for the opposite of 'necessary,' say 'unnecessary.'

For 'sense', answer 'nonsense'.

For 'happy', say 'unhappy'.

For 'believe,' say 'disbelieve'.

Encouraged, my friend decided to give it his best shot and hope for the best with enormous confidence and positivity. He went on chanting un, non, dis; un, non, dis...

The next day, he faced the exam with confidence. His answers for "opposites" went like this:

Fast - un fast

Happy - non-happy

Bright - this bright

Generous - ungenerous

Fresh - non-fresh

Firm - this firm

He somehow passed the SSLC exam with thirty-five marks in English (only God knows how!), and today, he's a successful salesman! He speaks fluent English and now knows that there is more to opposites than just un, non, and dis...!

150. Next Year's Strategy: Winning by Losing!

Dad: What happened in the cycle race?

Son: I came first in the "slow cycle race" and last in the "high-speed cycle race"

Dad: "So, where are the medals and certificates?!"

Son: Dad, "In the 'slow cycle race' I reached first, so no prize for that and in 'high-speed cycle race' I reached last; so, no prize for that too."

But dad, I will ensure that in the next year's competition I will reverse the results! I will come last in first and first in last!

His dad got totally lost!

151. Beyond the Catch: Finding Fulfilment in Simplicity

A small boat was docked in a tranquil Kovalam fishing village. A tourist, admiring the quality of the fish, asked the local fishermen how long it took them to catch their haul.

"Not very long," they replied in unison.

"Why don't you stay out longer and catch more?" the tourist inquired.

The fishermen explained that their small catches were enough to meet their needs and those of their families.

"But what do you do with the rest of your time?" the tourist pressed.

"We sleep in, fish a little, play with our children, and take siestas with our wives. In the evenings, we go into the village to see our friends, have a few drinks, play guitar, and sing a few songs. We live a full life," the fishermen responded.

The tourist, eager to offer advice, interrupted, "I have an MBA from Harvard, and I can help you! You should start by fishing longer every day. With the extra fish you catch, you can sell more and use the revenue to buy a bigger boat."

"And after that?" the fishermen asked.

"With the bigger boat, you could catch even more fish, and with the extra profits, you could buy a second boat, then a third, and eventually a fleet of trawlers. Instead of selling your fish to a middleman, you could negotiate directly with the processing plants or even open your own plant. Eventually, you could leave this small village and move to Cochin, Trivandrum, or Chennai, where you could oversee your growing empire."

"How long would this take?" asked the fishermen.

"Twenty, maybe twenty-five years," replied the tourist.

"And after that?" the fishermen asked again.

"That's when it gets really exciting!" the tourist exclaimed. "You could start buying and selling stocks, and before you know it, you'd be making millions!"

"Millions? Really? And after that?" the fishermen persisted.

"After that, you could retire, move to a small village by the coast, sleep in, play with your children, fish a little, take siestas with your wife, and spend your evenings enjoying drinks and the company of your friends," the tourist concluded.

The fishermen, puzzled, replied, "But sir, that's exactly what we're doing now. So why spend twenty-five years to get to where we already are?"

The moral of the story:

Know where you're headed in life—you might have already arrived there! Often, we forget that money isn't everything. Money is a means, not an end. There is more to life than just money!

152. The Miracle of Kindness

A woman approached a man sitting on the ground and greeted him with a warm, "Good morning." The man slowly looked up, noticing her expensive coat and well-fed appearance. She was clearly someone who had never known hunger. His first thought was that she, like many others, had come to mock him. "Leave me alone," he growled.

To his surprise, the woman remained standing, her smile revealing perfectly even, white teeth. "Are you hungry?" she asked.

"No," he replied sarcastically. "I just had lunch with the president. Now, go away."

Her smile widened, and before he knew it, she was gently lifting his arm. "What are you doing, lady?" he demanded angrily. "I told you to leave me alone."

Just then, a policeman approached. "Is there a problem, ma'am?" he asked.

"No problem, officer," the woman replied. "I'm just trying to help this man to his feet. Could you give me a hand?"

The officer scratched his head. "That's old Jack. He's been around here for a couple of years. What do you want with him?"

The woman pointed to a nearby cafeteria. "I'm going to get him something to eat and out of the cold for a while."

"Are you crazy, lady?" Jack protested. "I don't want to go in there!" But the officer, strong and resolute, grabbed Jack's other arm and helped lift him. "Let me go, officer. I didn't do anything."

"This is a good deal for you, Jack," the officer said. "Don't blow it,"

With some effort, the woman and the officer guided Jack into the cafeteria and sat him at a table in a quiet corner. It was mid-morning, so most of the breakfast crowd had left, and the lunch rush hadn't yet begun.

The manager walked over, eyeing the scene suspiciously. "What's going on here, officer?" he asked. "Is this man in trouble?"

"This lady brought him in to be fed," the officer explained.

"Not in here!" the manager snapped. "Having someone like him here is bad for business."

Old Jack grinned a toothless smile. "See, lady? I told you so. Now let me go. I didn't want to come here in the first place."

The woman turned to the manager and smiled. "Sir, are you familiar with Eddy and Associates, the banking firm down the street?"

"Of course," the manager replied, irritated. "They hold their weekly meetings in one of my banquet rooms."

"And do you make a good amount of money catering to those meetings?"

"What business is that of yours?" he asked, growing more impatient.

"I, sir, am Penelope Eddy, President and CEO of the company."

"Oh," the manager responded, his tone softening.

The woman smiled again. "I thought that might make a difference." She glanced at the officer, who was trying not to laugh. "Would you like to join us for a cup of coffee and a meal, officer?"

"No thanks, ma'am," the officer replied. "I'm on duty."

"How about a cup of coffee to go, then?"

"Yes, ma'am. That would be nice,"

The manager, eager to make amends, said, "I'll get your coffee right away, officer."

As the manager walked away, the officer remarked, "You certainly put him in his place."

"That wasn't my intent," the woman replied. "Believe it or not, I have a reason for all this."

She sat down across from Jack, who looked at her in disbelief. "Jack, do you remember me?"

Jack squinted, searching her face. "You do look familiar."

"I might be a bit older now," she said. "Maybe I've filled out a bit more since the days when you worked here, and I walked through that door, cold and hungry."

"Ma'am?" the officer asked, puzzled. He found it hard to believe that such a well-dressed woman could have ever been hungry.

"I had just graduated from college," the woman began. "I came to the city looking for a job, but I couldn't find anything. Eventually, I ran out of money and got kicked out of my apartment. I wandered the streets for days. It was February, and I was cold and starving. I saw this place and came in, hoping for something to eat."

Jack's face brightened with recognition. "I remember now! I was behind the counter. You asked if you could work for food, but I said it was against company policy."

"Yes," the woman continued. "Then you made me the biggest roast beef sandwich I had ever seen, gave me a cup of coffee, and told me to sit in a corner and enjoy it. I was afraid you'd get in trouble. But when I saw you pay for my food out of your own pocket, I knew things would be okay."

"So, you started your own business?" Jack asked.

"That very afternoon, I found a job. I worked my way up and eventually started my own business, which, with God's help, has prospered." She reached into her purse and pulled out a business card. "When you're finished here, I want you to visit Mr. Lyons, our personnel director. I'll talk to him, and I'm sure he can find something for you to do at the office. He might even advance you some money to buy clothes and find a place to stay until you get back on your feet. If you ever need anything, my door is always open."

Tears welled up in Jack's eyes. "How can I ever thank you?" he asked.

"Don't thank me," the woman said softly. "Thank God. He led me to you."

Outside the cafeteria, the officer and the woman paused before parting ways.

"Thank you for your help, officer," she said.

"On the contrary, Ms. Eddy," he replied. "Thank you. I witnessed a miracle today, something I'll never forget. And thank you for the coffee."

God calls us to "sow" good deeds, and in due time, we will "reap the rewards," perhaps when we need them most. We never know what lies ahead, so keep sowing "kindness" to those in need.

153. Catching Monkeys: An Analogy of the Stock Market

Once upon a time in a village, a man announced that he would buy monkeys for Rs 10 each. Seeing that the forest was teeming with monkeys, the villagers eagerly set out to catch as many as they could. The man bought thousands of monkeys at Rs 10 each, but as the supply dwindled, the villagers lost interest and stopped catching them.

To revive their enthusiasm, the man declared that he would now pay Rs 20 per monkey. Enticed by the higher price, the villagers returned to the forest with renewed energy. However, as the number of monkeys continued to dwindle, the villagers eventually went back to their farms.

Determined to get more monkeys, the man increased his offer to Rs. 25. But by this time, monkeys had become so rare that it was a challenge just to spot one, let alone catch it. Finally, the man announced that he would pay Rs. 50 per monkey.

Just as excitement reached its peak, the man had to leave for the city on business, leaving his assistant in charge of buying the monkeys. While the man was away, the assistant approached the villagers with a tempting offer: "Look at all these monkeys in the big cage that the man has collected. I'll sell them to you for Rs 35 each. When the man returns, you can sell them back to him for Rs 50."

Eager to make a profit, the villagers pooled all their savings and bought every monkey. But after that, they never saw the man or his assistant again—only the monkeys were left.

Welcome to the 'stock market'.

154. Faith and Fortitude: A Soldier's Tale

A group of fifteen soldiers, led by their Major Sahib, was on their way to a post in the Himalayas, where they would be stationed for the next three months. Another group, eagerly awaiting their arrival, would finally be relieved and return to the safety of their unit—some heading home to reunite with their families.

The soldiers were glad to be relieving their comrades who had completed their duty. The climb, however, was treacherous, and the journey wouldn't end until the following evening. Cold winter winds and intermittent snowfall made the trek even more gruelling.

"If only someone could offer us a cup of tea," the major thought wistfully, knowing it was a futile hope.

After another hour of trudging through the snow, they stumbled upon a dilapidated structure that resembled a small shop. But it was locked, and with no houses nearby, there was no way to find the owner in the middle of the night. For security reasons, it wasn't safe to knock on any doors either.

"It's a stalemate," the major sighed. "No tea, boys—bad luck."

He instructed his men to rest since they had been walking for over three hours. One of the soldiers, however, noticed something. "Sir, this does look like a tea shop, and we could make tea ourselves. But we'd have to break the lock."

The major hesitated, weighing the decision. A steaming cup of tea sounded tempting, especially in the biting cold. After a brief moment of reflection, he gave the order to break the lock.

They were in luck. The shop had everything needed to prepare tea, along with a few packets of biscuits. The soldiers brewed tea, and the warm drink brought immense relief as they huddled together in the cold night. Re-energised, they prepared to continue their journey.

But the major couldn't shake off a nagging thought—they had broken into the shop and consumed the goods without the owner's permission. They were not thieves; they were disciplined soldiers. The major knew they had to make it right.

Before leaving, the major took out a Rs 1000 note from his wallet and placed it under the sugar container on the counter, making sure the shop owner would find it first thing in the morning. Feeling a sense of relief, he ordered the move.

Days, weeks and months passed. The soldiers carried out their duties with bravery and were fortunate not to lose anyone in the intense insurgency they faced.

Then, the time came for them to be replaced by another brave group. On their way back, they stopped at the same shop, now open with the owner, an old man of modest means, standing behind the counter. He was delighted to see the fifteen soldiers, hoping to sell them tea.

As they sipped their tea, they chatted with the old man about his life, selling tea in such a remote and harsh location. The old man, full of stories, spoke of his faith in God. One soldier, curious, asked, "If there is a God, why would He leave you in such a poor condition?"

The old man smiled. "No, Sahib, don't say that. God exists—I have proof. A few months ago, I was going through very tough times. My only son had been severely beaten by terrorists who wanted information he didn't have. I had to close the shop early and take him to the hospital. There were medicines to buy, but I had no money. No one would lend me any, out of fear of the terrorists. I was hopeless, Sahib.

"That day, I prayed to Allah for help. And Sahib, Allah walked into my shop."

"When I returned to my shop and saw the lock broken, I thought someone had stolen whatever little I had. But then I saw that Allah had left Rs 1000 under the sugar pot. Sahib, you can't imagine what that money meant to me that day. Allah exists, Sahib, He truly does."

The faith in the old man's eyes was unwavering. The soldiers looked at their major, who silently conveyed his order: "Say nothing."

The major stood up, paid the bill, and hugged the old man. "Yes, Baba, I know—God does exist. And yes, the tea was wonderful."

As they left, fifteen pairs of eyes noticed the moisture gathering in the major's eyes—a rare sight.

The real truth is that any one of us can be a god to somebody.

155. Self-Worth: Unchanged by Life's Trials

It happened some years ago, but I remember the evening as if it were just last week. I was sitting in an audience, listening to a motivational speaker. During his talk, the speaker pulled out his wallet and held up a five-hundred-rupee note.

"Who wants this five-hundred-rupee note?" he asked.

A lot of hands shot up, including mine. As people began shouting, "Me! Me!" I wondered who the lucky person would be. And, like many others, I was curious—why would he simply give away five hundred rupees?

As the calls of "I want it!" grew louder, I noticed a young woman running down the aisle. She hurried onto the stage, approached the speaker, and snatched the five-hundred-rupee note from his hand.

"Well done, young lady," the speaker said into the microphone. "Most of us just wait for good things to happen. That's of no use. You've got to make things happen."

The speaker's words have stayed with me ever since: "Simply thinking about doing something is of no use."

Our lives are much like that. We all see opportunities around us and desire the good things in life. But the problem is, we often don't take action. We want the five hundred rupees on offer, but we hesitate. We gaze at it longingly, but we don't make the move.

The lesson is clear: Get up and do something about it. Don't worry about what others might think—take action.

Years later, I attended another event with a different motivational speaker. As I watched him pull out a five-hundred-rupee note and hold it up, I thought I knew what was coming. But this time, he asked a simple question, "How much is this worth?"

"Five hundred rupees," the crowd shouted in unison.

"Correct," the speaker said. Then he crumpled the note into a ball and asked, "How much is it worth now?"

"Five hundred rupees!" the audience yelled.

He then threw the note on the ground, stomped on it, and picked it up again. "And how much is it worth now?" he asked.

"Five hundred rupees!" the crowd responded once more.

"I want you to remember this," said the speaker. "Just because someone crumples it or steps on it, the value of the note does not change."

We should all strive to be like that five-hundred-rupee note.

In life, there will be times when we feel crushed, stepped on, and beaten down. But never let your self-worth diminish. Just because someone chooses to mistreat you, it doesn't change your worth in the slightest.

Don't allow your self-worth to diminish because of someone's harsh words or cruel actions.

156. Contentment over Possessions: Discovering Inner Joy

A Byte of Soul Food

There are two ways to be rich: One is to have everything you want, and the other is to be content with what you have. As we go through life, we inevitably either increase or diminish somebody's happiness.

A small house can hold as much happiness as a big one because true happiness comes from two things: what we can live without and what we cherish.

There's an old Eastern tale about a wealthy king who ruled a vast kingdom, lived in a grand palace, and had every luxury imaginable. Yet, despite all his power and possessions, he was deeply unhappy. Among his court was a wise sage, whose advice the king often sought in times of trouble. The king summoned the sage and asked how he might rid himself of his anxiety and despair—how he might truly find happiness, for he was sick in both body and mind. The sage responded, "There is but one cure for Your Majesty. You must sleep one night in the shirt of a happy man."

The king sent messengers throughout his realm to find a truly happy person. But every person they approached had some sorrow or misery that kept them from complete happiness. Finally, they came across a poor beggar sitting by the roadside, smiling contentedly. When asked if he was truly happy and free of sorrows, he confessed that he was indeed a happy man. The messengers then told him of their mission: the king must sleep one night in the shirt of a happy man and had offered a large sum of money for such a shirt. The beggar burst into laughter and replied, "I'm sorry, but I can't help the king. I don't even own a shirt!"

If you cannot find happiness along the way, you won't find it at the end of the road.

Happiness isn't something you hold in your hands; it's something you carry in your heart.

157. Cow and the Pig: Lesson in True Giving

Once, a wealthy landlord approached a priest and asked, "Why do people call me stingy when everyone knows that I will leave all my possessions to the church when I die?"

The priest replied with a story: "In this village, there lived a pig and a cow. The cow was beloved by everyone, while the pig was quite unpopular. This made the pig curious. He turned to the cow and said, 'People admire your kind nature and generous spirit. They appreciate you because you provide them with milk, butter, and cheese every day. But what about me? I offer them everything I have—delicious sausages, bacon, and ham. I even supply the ingredients for savoury sorpotel. Yet, no one seems to like me. Why is that?"

The priest continued, "Do you know how the cow responded?"

The cow replied, "Perhaps it's because I give all that I have while I am still alive."

158. When Cultures Collide: Prayers and Preferences

Grandmother was pretending to be deep in prayer, but her prayer beads were moving at lightning speed. This meant she was either excited or upset.

Mother put down the phone. "Some American girl from his office. She's coming to stay with us for a week." Her voice carried a sense of dread.

Father, however, had no such ambiguity. He knew the worst was on its way. He'd spent a year matching horoscopes, but my brother Vivek had found countless excuses to avoid visiting India, meeting the shortlisted Aiyer girls, or making any progress in advancing father's plans. Father always wore two parallel lines of sacred ash on his forehead. Now there were four, so deep were the worry lines etched into his skin.

Vijayanthi sat in a corner, supposedly engrossed in a book, but secretly texting her brother with a vivid play-by-play of the scene unfolding before her.

A few days later, Vijayanthi was standing outside the airport with her father. He tried hard not to make eye contact with any of the American women passing by. Vijayanthi held up a sign that read "Barbara."

Finally, a large woman stepped out, waving enthusiastically and shouting, "Hi! Mr. Ayyer, how ARE you?"

Everyone turned to look at them. Father seemed to shrink visibly. Barbara took three long strides and wrapped him in a tight hug. Watching him awkwardly squirm out of it was too funny. Vijayanthi could hear him whispering, "Shiva, Shiva, Narayana."

She then turned to Vijayanthi and said, "You must be Vijayanthi." "Yes, Vijayanthi," she replied with a polite smile.

Suddenly, Vijayanthi's dull existence in Madurai seemed poised to become much more interesting. For the next week, at least, life promised to be anything but boring for her!

Soon, they had all gathered for lunch at home. Barbara had changed into an even shorter skirt, and the plunging neckline of her blouse was right in line with father's shocked gaze. He glared at mother as if she were responsible for all the family's problems.

Barbara asked, "Do you only eat vegetarian food? Always?" as if the concept was completely foreign to her.

"You know what really goes well with Indian food, especially chicken? Indian beer!" she added with a smile, oblivious to the furious look on father's face and the choking sounds coming from mother. Vijayanthi stifled her laughter.

Everyone was trying to gather information without asking the one question on all our minds: What exactly was the nature of the relationship between Vivek and Barbara?

After lunch, Barbara pulled out a laptop. "I have some pictures of Vivek," she said.

They all crowded around. The first picture was harmless—Vivek in shorts, standing alone on a beach. But the next one was a shocker. Vivek was on the beach again, but this time with Barbara draped all over him, wearing a skimpy bikini and lovingly wrapping her hand around his neck.

Father stood up and flicked the thin towel off his shoulder, a gesture that everyone in the family had learned to fear. He rushed to the door and stormed out.

Barbara commented, "It must be hard for Mr. Aayyer. He must miss his son."

We didn't have the heart to tell her that if Vivek had been within father's reach, that neck she'd wrapped her hand around might have been in serious danger.

Vijayanth's parents and grandmother seemed to come to an unspoken agreement. They would deal with Vivek later. For now, Barbara was a foreign guest and needed to be treated with respect. But Barbara didn't make that easy. Soon, mother had a permanent frown, and father looked like he was paying off some past-life karma.

Vivek had told us he would be at a conference in Jakarta all week and wouldn't be available by phone or email. But Barbara had long, lovey-dovey conversations with two other men—one named Steve and another named Keith. We all strained to hear every word. "I miss you!" she said to both.

She also kept talking about Vivek and the places they'd visited together, with pictures to back it up.

This was the best entertainment Vijayanthi had in a long time—better even than the day her cousin eloped with a Telugu Christian girl. My aunt had burst through the door, howling, only to faint dramatically onto their plush sofa.

Father had said that if it had been his son, the door would have been shut in his face forever.

Aunt had promptly revived and retorted, "You'll understand when it's your son!" How she would have laughed if she knew about Barbara!

On the fifth day of Barbara's visit, the family was jolted awake by the sound of her vomiting. The bathroom door was closed, water running, but the sound of Barbara crying and vomiting at the same time was unmistakable. Mother and grandmother exchanged worried glances. Barbara emerged, her face red.

"I don't know why," she said, "but I feel queasy in the mornings now."

If she'd seen as many Indian movies as Vijayanthi had, she'd know why. Mother stood frozen. Should she respond with the compassion reserved for a pregnant woman? Or the criticism reserved for a pregnant unmarried woman? Or the fear reserved for a pregnant, unmarried, foreign woman who could embroil one's son in a paternity suit? Mother, who usually navigated the currents of married life like a seasoned sailor, now seemed completely adrift. She seemed to hope that if she didn't react, it might all just disappear like a bad dream.

Vijayanthi made a mental note not to leave the house for the next week. Whatever her parents would say to Vivek when they finally got hold of him was going to be too interesting to miss. But to her disappointment, they never got the chance.

The day Barbara was supposed to leave, they received a brief email from Vivek. "Sorry, still stuck in Jakarta. Just wanted to mention, another friend of mine, Sameera Sheikh, needs a place to stay. She'll be arriving from Hyderabad tomorrow at 10 a.m. Sorry for the trouble."

So, there we were again, father and I, standing outside the airport with a sign that read "Sameera".

Finally, a young woman in a salwar-kameez noticed the sign, smiled slightly, and walked quietly toward us. When she did a 'Namaste' to father, I saw his eyes well up. She took my hand warmly and said, "Hello, Vyjayanthi, I've heard so much about you." Vyjayanthi instantly liked her.

In the car, father was unusually friendly. Sameera and Vivek had been part of the same friend group at Ohio University. She now worked as a child psychologist.

She didn't seem too bad at family psychology either. She brought a shawl for grandmother, a saree for mother, and Hyderabadi bangles for Vijayanthi.

"Just some small gifts. I have to meet a professor at Madurai University, and it's so kind of you to let me stay," she said. The mood in the house lifted instantly.

Even grandmother smiled.

At lunch, Sameera said, "This is delicious. When I make sambar, it comes out like chhole, and my chhole tastes just like sambar!"

Mother smiled. "Oh, just watch for two days and you'll get the hang of it."

Grandmother had never allowed a Muslim into the kitchen, but mother seemed to have taken charge, deciding who was worthy of entering.

Sameera was respectful enough to avoid the puja room. But on the third day, Vijayanthi was stunned to see father inviting her in, showing her the idols passed down from his father.

"God is one," he said to her. Sameera nodded wisely.

By the fifth day, a collective thought seemed to form in the family's mind. If Vivek had to choose his own bride, why couldn't it be someone like Sameera?

On the sixth day, when Vivek called from the airport to say he'd cut his Jakarta trip short and was on his way home, everyone had a million things to discuss with him.

Vivek arrived by taxi just as Sameera had gone to the university.

"So, how was Barbara's visit?" he asked casually.

"How did you meet her?" Mother asked sternly.

"She's my secretary," he said. "She works really hard and would do anything to help," he turned and winked at Vijayanthi.

By the time Sameera returned that evening, it was almost as if the grandmother and parents had come up with the idea themselves that she should join the family.

"Don't worry about anything. Just tell us if you're willing to marry Vivek," they said to Sameera. "We'll speak to your parents."

On the wedding day, a huge bouquet arrived at the Mandapam. The tag read:

Flight to India - $1300

Indian kurta - $5

Emetic to throw up - $1

The look on your parents' faces – Priceless! - As always, yours, Barbara!

159. When Cooking Mirrors Driving: A Hilarious Revelation

A wife was making breakfast, frying eggs for her husband. Suddenly, her husband burst into the kitchen.

"Careful... CAREFUL!! Add more butter! Oh my gosh, you're cooking too many at once. TOO MANY!! Flip them! FLIP THEM NOW!! We need more butter. Oh my gosh, WHERE are we going to get MORE BUTTER?! They're going to STICK!! Careful... CAREFUL!! I said be CAREFUL!! You NEVER listen to me when you're cooking! Never!! Flip them! HURRY UP!! Are you CRAZY? Have you lost your mind? Don't forget the salt. You always forget the salt. Use the salt. USE THE SALT! THE SALT!!"

The wife stared at him. "What the hell is wrong with you? You think I don't know how to fry a couple of eggs?"

The husband calmly replied, "I just wanted to show you what it feels like when I'm driving."

160. The Silent Exodus: The Role of Managers in Retaining Talented People

Every company faces the challenge of employees leaving for better pay or opportunities.

Earlier this year, Raman, a senior software designer, received an offer from a prestigious international firm to work in its India operations, developing specialised software. He was ecstatic.

He had heard great things about the CEO. The salary was impressive, and the company had everything: employee-friendly HR policies, a brand-new office, cutting-edge technology, and even a canteen that served excellent food.

Twice, Raman was sent abroad for training. "My learning curve has never been sharper," he remarked soon after joining.

Yet, last week, less than eight months after he started, Raman quit.

Why would a talented employee like Raman leave?

Raman's reason for leaving is the same one that drives many skilled people away.

The answer can be found in one of the largest studies conducted by the Gallup Organisation. This study, which surveyed over a million employees and 80,000 managers, was published in the book "First, Break All the Rules." It revealed a surprising insight:

If you're losing good people, look at their immediate boss. The immediate boss is the reason people stay and thrive in a company, and also the reason they leave. When people leave, they take their knowledge, experience, and contacts with them—often to the competition.

"People leave managers, not companies."

Do managers drive people away?

HR experts say that of all the forms of mistreatment, employees find "humiliation" the most unbearable. The first time it happens, an employee might not leave, but a seed is planted. The second time, the thought grows. The third time, they start looking for another job.

When people can't openly express their anger, they resort to passive aggression—by slowing down, doing only what's required, and withholding crucial information. As one employee says, "If you work for a jerk, you basically want to see them fail. Your heart and soul aren't in the job."

Different managers stress employees in different ways—by being too controlling, too suspicious, too pushy, or too critical. But they forget that workers aren't fixed assets; they're free agents. When this goes on too long, an employee will eventually quit—often over something trivial.

Talented people leave. Others stay until they get an opportunity.

161. A Comical Cultural Clash

An Army Colonel was visiting a temple in South India when the priest approached him and quietly asked, "Gotram?"

With a wink, the Colonel replied, he understood the question as "Got Rum?" "Yes, in my car—two bottles of Old Monk, Bacardi, and Black Dog whiskey."

The priest's face turned red with anger, and he told the Colonel to leave immediately.

Realising what had gone wrong, the Colonel's wife nudged him and whispered, "He was asking about your Gotram (गोत्रम)!" and look at what you have said!"

162. The 25/75 Rule: Understanding Success and Failure

Once, a young man sat by the beach, feeling deeply troubled and contemplating ending his life.

As he wrestled with his despair, he suddenly heard a voice calling out, "Just one more time!" Turning around, he saw a group of athletes training. A young boy was striving to reach a target but had failed multiple times. Yet, his coach remained unwaveringly supportive. After nearly eighteen attempts, the boy finally succeeded, and the young man couldn't help but smile and cheer along with the other spectators.

Curious about the coach's calm demeanour and persistent encouragement, the young man approached him and asked how he managed to stay so positive. The coach replied, "Let me finish my session first, and I'll share my thoughts with you." After the training ended, the coach and the young man began walking together.

The coach then shared an interesting perspective: "Did you know that lions only succeed in about 25% of their hunting attempts? This means they fail 75% of the time, yet they never lose hope in their pursuit. Their perseverance isn't driven solely by hunger, but by an instinctual understanding of the 'Law of Wasted Efforts' that governs nature. For instance, half of all fish eggs are consumed, many baby bears don't survive to adulthood, most of the world's rain falls into the oceans, and countless seeds are eaten by birds before they can grow."

Scientists have discovered that animals, trees, and other natural forces intuitively accept this law of wasted efforts. In contrast, humans often view a lack of success in a few attempts as failure."

163. Reflections by Water: A Journey Through Time...

Walk With Me While I Age.

I hope this poem has the same effect on you as it did on me - then my publishing it will be worth the effort. Walk with me by the water - worth the read...

A BEAUTIFUL POEM ABOUT GROWING OLDER:

-

-

-

-

-

-

-

-

-

-

-

-

Oh my God!! "I forgot the words!"

164. New Year Wishes

May you receive a clean bill of health from your dentist, cardiologist, gastroenterologist, urologist, proctologist, podiatrist, psychiatrist, plumber, and the IT.

May your hair, teeth, face-lift, abs, and stocks stay firm; and may your blood pressure, triglycerides, cholesterol, white blood cell count, and mortgage interest remain low.

May New Year's Eve find you surrounded by beloved family and cherished friends, enjoying a meal that tastes better, a setting that's more peaceful, a cost that's more affordable, and a joy that's more fulfilling than anything else you might typically do that night.

May the reflection in your mirror bring you joy, and may others see in you what delights them. May someone love you enough to overlook your flaws, ignore your imperfections, and celebrate your virtues with the world.

May telemarketers wait until after dinner to call, commercials not be louder than the TV shows you're watching, and may your chequebook and budget balance—with room for generosity.

May you remember to say "I love you" every day to your spouse, child, parents, and siblings—but not to your secretary, nurse, masseuse, hairdresser, or tennis instructor!

And may we live in a world of peace, where God's love is evident in every sunset, every blossoming flower, every baby's smile, every lover's kiss, and every miraculous beat of our hearts.

165. A Cultural Encounter at Checkout

An Indian man moves to a western country and visits a supermarket. While shopping, he notices cat food on sale and picks up a dozen cans. When he gets to the checkout, the manager becomes suspicious, thinking the man might be buying the cat food to feed his kids instead. The manager asks him to show his cat before allowing the purchase. The Indian man goes home, returns with his cat, and is allowed to buy the cat food.

A week later, the Indian man sees dog food on special and picks up a dozen cans. Once again, the manager is suspicious, doubting that the man owns a dog. He asks him to bring in the dog to prove it. The Indian man goes home, returns with his dog, and is allowed to buy the dog food.

The following week, the Indian man returns to the supermarket with a bag in hand. He approaches the manager and asks him to reach into the bag. The manager hesitantly puts his hand inside, feeling something slimy, and quickly pulls it out, yelling, "What the hell is this? Is this...?"

The Indian man calmly replies, "Yes, it is. Now I'd like to buy some toilet paper."

166. The Pentium Plunge: A Modern Panchatantra

Once upon a time, there was a software engineer who spent his days developing programs on his trusty Pentium machine, sitting under a tree by the riverside. He made his living by selling these programs at the Sunday market. One day, as he worked, his computer accidentally fell off the table and plunged into the river.

Remembering the Panchatantra story from his childhood about the honest woodcutter and the axe, he decided to pray to the River Goddess for help.

The story goes that a poor man named Mangal earned his livelihood by cutting wood during the day and selling it in the market each evening. One day, while cutting a tree branch near a river, his axe slipped from his hands and fell into the water. Distraught, Mangal jumped into the river but couldn't find his axe. As he wept in despair, the Goddess of the forest appeared and asked why he was crying. After hearing his plight, the Goddess promised to retrieve his axe. She first brought out a gold axe and asked if it was his. Mangal, being honest, said it wasn't. She then brought out a silver axe, but again, Mangal refused, saying it wasn't his. Finally, she brought out his simple iron axe, and Mangal joyfully claimed it as his own. Pleased with his honesty, the Goddess rewarded him with all three axes, making him a wealthy man.

Inspired by this tale, the software engineer began praying to the River Goddess. After a month of dedicated prayers, the

Goddess finally appeared. He explained to her that his computer had fallen into the river.

The River Goddess, wanting to test his honesty, first showed him a matchbox and asked, "Is this your computer?" Disappointed by her lack of understanding, the engineer replied, "No." Next, she produced a pocket-sized calculator and asked if it was his. Irritated, the engineer responded, "No, definitely not!" Finally, the Goddess showed him his Pentium machine and asked if it was his. With no other option, the engineer sighed and admitted, "Yes."

The River Goddess was pleased with his honesty and was about to reward him with all three items when the engineer interrupted and said, "Aren't you supposed to show me better computers before giving me my own?"

Angered by his arrogance, the Goddess snapped, "I know that, you fool! The first two items I showed you were the Trillennium and the Billennium, the latest computers!" With that, she disappeared, taking the Pentium with her.

Moral of the story: If you're not up-to-date with technology trends, it's better to stay quiet and let others think you're a fool than to speak and remove all doubt!

167. Fast Cars and Faster Meters

A Japanese tourist hailed a taxi in downtown Delhi and asked to be taken to the international airport.

As they drove, a car sped past them. The tourist exclaimed, "Oh! TOYOTA! Made in Japan! Very fast!"

A little later, another car zoomed by. "Oh! NISSAN! Made in Japan! Very fast!"

Soon after, yet another car whizzed past. "Oh, Mitsubishi! Made in Japan! Very fast!"

The taxi driver, who was proudly Indian, was starting to get annoyed that these Japanese cars kept overtaking his taxi. Just as they were approaching the airport, another car zipped by. "Oh! Honda! Made in Japan! Very fast!"

The taxi driver pulled over, pointed to the meter and said, "That'll be 500 Rupees."

"500 Rupees? But it was such a short ride! Why so much?"

The taxi driver smiled and replied, "Taxi meter. Made in India. Very fast."

168. PhD in Humour

Sonali booked a cab from Mumbai airport to her home. When she arrived at her destination, she paid the fare. The driver thanked her and handed her his business card. It read:

Dr. Ramakanth Akula, PhD

Surprised, Sonali asked, "Wow! A driver with a PhD? That's incredible! Can you tell me why you're driving with such a high qualification?"

Ramakanth Akula smiled and explained, "Madam, 'Dr' stands for driver. The double PhD? The first PhD means 'privately hired driver,' and the second PhD means 'passed high school with difficulty!'"

Sonali had a hearty laugh and handsomely tipped Dr. Ramakanth Akula, PhD!

169. The Roots of Jealousy: Breaking Free from Comparison

Jealousy stems from comparison. Society has conditioned us to constantly measure ourselves against others—whether it's their homes, physical appearance, wealth, or charisma. This relentless comparison breeds jealousy, which is a natural outcome of such conditioning.

However, if we stop comparing ourselves to others, jealousy fades away. We begin to recognise our individuality; we are unique and do not need to be like anyone else. Just as it would be pointless to compare ourselves to trees or birds, we should not measure our worth against other people. Each person is distinct and incomparable. Once we embrace this truth, jealousy dissipates. You are you—no one else has ever been or will ever be like you.

God creates only originals, not duplicates.

Consider a humorous example: a group of chickens watches a football land in their yard. One rooster observes, "I'm not complaining, girls, but look at the work they are turning out next door." This reflects a common sentiment—everyone seems to have it better than us. We often assume that our neighbours are happier, more successful, or more fulfilled. Yet, they might be looking at us with the same envy.

This cycle of comparison leads to collective misery. An elderly farmer, witnessing the aftermath of a flood, learns that his neighbours have also lost their pigs. Instead of despair, he feels a sense of relief: "It isn't as bad as I thought." This illustrates how shared suffering can bring a strange comfort.

But why do we let the lives of others affect us? It's because we fail to nurture our own happiness and allow our inner joy to flourish. When we feel empty inside, we look outward, focusing on others' exteriors—often polished and deceptive—while we know our own inner turmoil.

An ancient Sufi tale illustrates this point. A man burdened by his suffering prayed to God, wishing to exchange his pain for someone else's. In a dream, God invited everyone to bring their suffering to the temple and choose anew. When faced with the reality of others' burdens, the man rushed to reclaim his own, realising that familiarity with his pain was preferable to the unknown.

The lesson here is profound: nothing had changed, yet everyone returned home content. The man thanked God for the revelation, understanding that his suffering was meant for him.

Jealousy causes constant suffering, leading to meanness and phoniness. We often pretend to be something we are not, imitating others instead of embracing our true selves. This artificiality stems from jealousy and competition.

Consider the absurdity of trying to keep up with others. For instance, Jim and Nancy Smith returned from a lavish European vacation, only to be embarrassed by the contents of their luggage—filled with wigs, silk underwear, and perfume. This illustrates how we sometimes hide behind superficialities, driven by jealousy.

To escape this cycle, we must cultivate our inner treasures. Embrace authenticity and love yourself as you are. By doing so, the doors to genuine happiness will open. They have always been available; we just need to be willing to see them.

170. Gratitude and Giggles

I called my teachers to thank them and said, "I am what I am today because of you."

Teachers said, "Don't blame us; we tried our best!"

171. The Pen and the Purse: A Lesson on the Value of Knowledge Over Wealth

In an English language question paper, the following essay topic was presented:

"Crores of rupees can be stolen from banks, but the pen at the counter, tied with a piece of twine, is never stolen! Elaborate on the implied message of this."

One student responded:

The implied message is quite clear. It suggests that while wealth (represented by Lakshmi) can be stolen, knowledge (represented by Saraswati) cannot. Instead of merely leaving behind material wealth for your children, it is far better to provide them with education—broad knowledge across many subjects and deeper expertise in one or two areas.

It is crucial to teach children how to manage emotions, relationships, handle finances, cope with stress, face adversity, deal with failure, and above all, understand spirituality, which is the foundation of everything.

This valuable lesson can be learned from a bank - "the pen tied to a twine!" With education, you can acquire money, but with money, you cannot buy education.

You can inherit wealth but cannot inherit knowledge.

172. Money as a Magnifier: Amplifying the True Essence of Character

Does money change people? Do they become different when they acquire lots of money?

The answer is NO.

But what does money really do?

Money amplifies who people already are.

If someone is foolish and unlikeable, having more money will only make them a bigger fool and even more unlikeable.

If they're stingy, wealth will make them even more miserly.

On the flip side, if someone is generous, more money will make them even more giving, empathetic, and compassionate.

Money acts as a magnifier, bringing out the "true you" even more clearly when wealth increases.

173. The Jalebi Contest's Bitter Twist

There was an eating competition in the city—specifically a jalebi-eating contest, where each jalebi had a 3-inch diameter. The prize was Rs 50,000, with an entry fee of Rs 500. The challenge: whoever could eat 100 jalebis in 15 minutes would win.

Saketh, a man known for his ability to eat 100 jalebis within the time limit, had his participation sponsored by his wealthy friend, Naveen. Confident in Saketh's skills, Naveen bragged to everyone about his friend's talent, saying Saketh would easily down 100 jalebis in 15 minutes.

The competition was set for Sunday at 4 pm, and it drew many participants. Groups of five contestants at a time were called to the table, where referees counted the jalebis consumed. In the first round, participants struggled to eat more than 20 or 25 jalebis. The overwhelming sweetness caused dizziness, and many had to stop well before reaching the target.

Then, it was Saketh's turn. All eyes were on him as Naveen's boasts echoed in the air. Saketh started strong, devouring thirty jalebis quickly. He powered through to 35, then 40, and forty-five. But suddenly, he began to slow down. At 50, he showed signs of discomfort, and by 60, he was visibly struggling.

Naveen cheered him on, shouting, "Come on, only forty more to go, and just 3 minutes left!" But Saketh, dazed and sluggish, could only manage ten more jalebis in the next two minutes and just three in the final minute. In total, he consumed seventy-three jalebis—far ahead of the other participants, but short of the 100-mark.

The crowd, having expected more, started mocking Naveen for his misplaced confidence. Embarrassed, Naveen approached Saketh and said, "I had so much faith in you! I've seen you eat 100 jalebis in 15 minutes before. What happened today?"

Saketh, still recovering, replied, "I did well in practice this morning!... ate all 100 jalebis then!"

174. Serendipity - A Journey of Connection

My wife and I were travelling on the Cholan Express, returning from the temple town of Kumbakonam to Chennai. It was a day train with berths available. I climbed onto the upper berth with a storybook in hand, ready to enjoy some reading.

Meanwhile, my wife struck up a conversation with a fellow female passenger. They chatted like old friends, discussing their families, relationships, careers, aspirations, health, and more. I listened in on parts of their conversation, read my book, and even dozed off for a bit. Before we reached Chennai, my wife invited her new friend to stay in touch and come over for dinner sometime. The woman was grateful and extended the same invitation, insisting that my wife visit her home first, to which my wife happily agreed.

As we made our way home, I asked my wife if she had taken down the copassenger's phone number. She smiled and said no.

175. Contrasting Workspaces

When you go to a salon, you find a lot of hair

When we go to a mechanic's shed, we find a lot of oil, nuts, and bolts.

When you go to a tailor's shop, we find rolls of fabric, thread, needles.

I wonder why people in banks are so indifferent!

176. Written Outside a Hospital's Outpatient Department

When you cross 50 years of age, you must reduce your evening friends and increase your morning friends.

Response by a Patient:

"What rubbish!!

Who drinks so early in the morning!"

177. The Challenge of Effective Sequences

If you want a monkey to recite Shakespeare from the top of a 10-foot pedestal, what would you do first? The logical sequence is to train the monkey, which is the harder task, and then build the pedestal, the easier one. However, people often do the opposite – they build the pedestal first and then try to train the monkey. Why? Because they feel like they've completed 50% of the work and assume the rest will follow. But which task is truly more difficult: training the monkey or building the pedestal? The answer is obvious.

Our egos are so fragile that we often praise and reward the "monkey reciting Shakespeare team" for their progress just because they've built the pedestal first, even though it's the training, the harder and more essential part, that truly deserves the recognition!

178. Temporary Permanent Loan

We've often heard from wise people that the world operates on "Cause-and-Effect." We're encouraged to do good, expecting good in return, but we should also proceed with caution. I've learned this lesson the hard way, and here's my story:

In today's world of the internet, online banking, and ATMs, some of us "old-timers" still prefer visiting the bank to withdraw money. I've noticed that many people come to the bank well-prepared with cell phones, chargers, headphones, and power banks—but surprisingly, no one carries a pen. When I lend them mine, they never return it!

But I thought I'd outsmart them. Now, whenever someone asks for my pen, I cleverly remove the cap, keep it with me, and hand over only the pen, fully expecting it to come back.

Well, my brilliant plan didn't go as expected. I now have eighteen pen caps, but no pens!

179. The Clever Con

Heard this story from my friend: Two classmates were travelling by bus from Bengaluru to Chennai during a busy festival season. The buses were packed, and with no seats available, both friends had to stand for hours. After three hours of standing with no one getting off, and two more hours of travel still ahead, their legs began to ache.

Then, one of them had a clever idea. He shared it with his friend, and the show began. The first friend started coughing, drawing some attention from seated passengers, but nothing changed. His coughing grew louder, until finally, a passenger sitting in the aisle seat gave up his spot to the coughing friend.

The first friend continued coughing as the second one, feigning concern, asked about his recent blood test results. The first friend, playing along, replied, "I didn't want to tell you, but since you're asking, the report says I have TB."

The second friend, pretending to be alarmed, asked, "Is TB contagious?"

"Of course, yes," the first friend responded.

At this, the passenger sitting next to him quickly vacated the window seat, and the second friend slipped into it.

And just like that, the coughing stopped, and the two friends slept soundly, much to the astonishment of the other passengers!

180. When Donkeys Outsmart Meteorologists

The king decided to go fishing and asked the royal weather forecaster for the forecast over the next few hours. The palace meteorologist assured him that there was no chance of rain.

So, the King and Queen set out for their fishing trip. On their way, they encountered a fisherman riding a donkey with a fishing pole. The king asked the fisherman if the fish were biting.

The fisherman replied, "Your Majesty, you should return to the palace. A massive rainstorm is coming soon."

The king, trusting the palace meteorologist—whom he respected highly due to his education and high salary—dismissed the fisherman's warning and continued on his way.

Not long after, a torrential downpour drenched the King and Queen.

Furious, the king returned to the palace and dismissed the meteorologist. He then offered the position of royal forecaster to the fisherman.

The fisherman said, "Your Majesty, I don't actually know anything about forecasting. I just get my information from my donkey. When I see his ears drooping, I know it's going to rain."

So, the king hired the donkey.

And thus began the tradition of appointing less-than-qualified individuals to influential positions everywhere—a practice that continues to this day!

181. A Dream of Gratitude

Goddess Mahalakshmi appeared in the man's dream and said, "I know you have been happy for this long, and I have provided you with enough and more wealth to take care of your needs for the future; but according to your horoscope, I have to leave you to go to other places; however, she asked if he needed to say something."

The man did not panic but thanked her for all the blessings out of deep gratitude and said, "All I need is a happy home and all my people should be happy, feeling secure and pleased with themselves."

Goddess Lakshmi replied, "I am very happy with your nicely thought-out selfless answer; I stay in places where there is harmony, the gift of understanding, and contentment; I have changed my plans; I have decided to stay back!"

182. Defining Success Through Diverse Lenses

Success means different things to different people, shaped by their unique circumstances and stages in life. During a debate on the topic "What is success?", various opinions emerged.

One person said, "Success is studying hard, going to the U.S., pursuing higher studies, securing a Green Card, getting married, and settling down there."

Another person shared, "For me, it's about studying well, passing the UPSC exams, landing in an administrative job, buying a nice house, and establishing a stable life."

Someone else said, "Success means studying well, starting a business, making a lot of money, and achieving financial security."

Yet another view was, "I want to be like my father or mother when I grow up—emulating their morals, ethics, selflessness, kindness, contribution to society, justice, and integrity after completing my education."

In the end, success for many parents is when their children say, "I want to be like my father or mother when I grow up."

183. Finding Tranquillity Amidst Chaos

We often talk about tranquillity, but it's not just about being in a quiet, peaceful place like a retreat, a hill station, or a cosy resort, or even a walk in the woods. Those are external sources of calm. While we may visit such places occasionally, the reality is that most of us spend our time in noisy environments—markets, offices, hospitals, or courts—where the external noise can be overwhelming.

True tranquillity, however, comes from within. It requires a calm heart and the ability to concentrate on what truly matters, no matter the external circumstances. To achieve this, we must focus on the task at hand, ignoring distractions.

One effective way to maintain focus is by listing your tasks—on paper or digitally—and prioritising them. Take on one task at a time, and even when multitasking is necessary, deeply focus on one task before moving to the next.

Here's a story to reflect on:

Once upon a time, a young disciple seeking enlightenment set out on a journey to visit a famous Zen Master, renowned for his wisdom. After travelling for days, crossing mountains and valleys, the disciple finally arrived at the simple home of the master. Filled with anticipation, he approached and said, "Master, please teach me the secret to finding inner peace and tranquillity."

The Zen Master smiled warmly and gestured for the disciple to follow him. They walked together in silence until they reached a small teahouse in the heart of a bustling marketplace. As they entered, the disciple became acutely aware of the surrounding chaos—merchants shouting, customers haggling, and the general clamour of a busy market.

Without a word, the Zen Master sat down at a table and motioned for the disciple to join him. A server came over and asked, "What can I get for you?" The master simply replied, "Two cups of tea, please."

As they waited, the disciple found himself overwhelmed by the noise. Unable to contain his frustration, he turned to the master and asked, "Master, how can anyone find peace in the midst of all this chaos? The noise is unbearable."

The Zen Master smiled gently and asked, "Tell me, what do you hear?"

The disciple listened and replied, "I hear the merchants shouting, customers bargaining, and the clatter of dishes."

The master nodded. "And what do you see?"

The disciple looked around. "People rushing, colourful goods everywhere, and the busyness of the marketplace."

The Zen Master smiled again and said, "Now, focus on our table. What do you hear?"

The disciple turned his attention to their immediate surroundings, listening closely. To his surprise, the noise of the marketplace seemed to fade. "Master, I can only hear the tea being prepared. The noise from outside has disappeared,"

The Zen Master nodded approvingly. "You see, my dear disciple, this is the power of ignoring. When you focus on what truly matters and let go of unnecessary distractions, you create your own peace. The noise of the world will always be there, but it's up to you to choose what enters your mind and heart."

The disciple's eyes widened with understanding. He realised that peace wasn't about silencing the world, but about changing his own focus. From that moment, he understood that inner peace comes not from changing the outside world, but from changing his perception and where he places his attention.

Grateful for the wisdom he had received, the disciple continued his journey, learning to ignore the noise of the world and cultivate inner peace. He carried with him the master's lesson: that the power of ignoring is not about turning a blind eye to life, but about consciously choosing where to direct one's thoughts and energy. By focusing on what truly matters, one can find peace and clarity, even amidst chaos.

184. Doctor Phobia

Lecturer: What would you do if you fell ill? Would you see a doctor?

Student: I wouldn't go to the doctor.

Lecturer: So, what would you do instead?

Student: I'd just lie down in bed!

Lecturer: Just lie down?

Student: No, I'd take off my clothes and lie down in bed!

Lecturer: Why would you do that? What makes you hesitant to see a doctor?

Student: It's because of my uncle.

Lecturer: What happened to him?

Student: He passed away.

Lecturer: Did he die from chest pain?

Student: No.

Lecturer: Then what caused his death?

Student: He died because of the doctor. The doctor examined him with a stethoscope, said everything was fine, and sent him away after collecting the consultation fee. But he died because of that doctor.

Lecturer: I'm having trouble following—did he die of a heart attack?

Student: A few minutes after seeing the doctor, my uncle was walking on the road when a car hit him.

Lecturer: So, what's the issue?

Student: "That doctor was driving the car!"

Lecturer: Oh my!

185. The Journey to Self-Discovery

RKN Mangal was a billionaire in the pharmaceutical industry, yet despite his wealth, he felt deeply unfulfilled. Friends advised him to learn meditation from a true master, believing it could bring him inner peace. After seeking recommendations, his closest aide informed him that Sage Rama, who lived in the Shivani mountains of the Himalayas, was considered the best teacher. Sage Rama was known for his constant communion with a higher power.

Mangal decided to make the journey, accompanied by a dozen well-dressed men in suits, ties, and polished shoes. He too dressed in his finest attire, reflecting his status. With much pomp, the group arrived at the sage's humble and tranquil hut, where Sage Rama sat peacefully, his eyes closed in deep meditation, a serene smile on his face, unaware of the bustling activity around him.

The sound of leaves rustling and the whispers of the men disturbed the sage's meditation. Slowly, he opened his eyes and saw the group before him. Mangal stepped forward, bowed respectfully, and greeted the sage with a "Namaste."

Sage Rama looked at him and asked, "What do you want?"

Mangal replied, "I want to learn meditation. People say you are the best teacher."

The sage then asked, "Who are you?"

Surprised, Mangal responded, "Don't you know? I am RKN Mangal."

The sage said calmly, "That's your name. Tell me who you are."

Mangal, a bit perplexed, replied, "I'm from ZEE Pharmaceuticals."

"That's your company's name. Tell me who you are," the sage repeated.

Mangal continued, "I am the Managing Director of the company."

"That's your job title. Tell me who you are," the sage asked again.

Frustrated, Mangal said, "Are you joking? Our company is on the Fortune 500 list."

"That's your company's status. Tell me who you are," the sage persisted.

Mangal, feeling cornered, said, "I graduated first from Stanford with an MBA."

"That's your education. Tell me who you are."

Mangal, now sweating, added, "My father founded the company from scratch in 1980."

"That's about your father. Who are you?" the sage asked once more.

"My son Deepak is the CEO of the company now," Mangal said, struggling.

The sage smiled and said, "I didn't ask about your son or descendants. I'm asking you: Who are you?"

With eleven pairs of eyes on him, Mangal, overwhelmed and confused, finally replied, "Master, I give up. I don't know who I am. I guess I am actually nothing."

The sage smiled warmly and said, "Now, that's a good place to begin. Let's start!"

186. Live VS Replay: Bhagyaraj's Insight on Love and Marriage

Bhagyaraj, a well-known film actor and director, travelled to Canada to participate in a programme. While there, he remembered that his former school teacher lived in Canada and decided to call him. The teacher was delighted to hear from his former student and warmly invited him to his home.

Upon visiting, the teacher mentioned that his son, Vijay, had a question for Bhagyaraj. Bhagyaraj, smiling, said, "Sir, you're my teacher, you could have easily answered the question." The teacher replied, "I've seen many of your films, and I know you have a unique perspective. I think you should give it a try." He then introduced Vijay to Bhagyaraj.

After some introductions, Vijay asked, "Uncle, I've noticed that in our country, arranged marriages are common and successful. Families meet, match horoscopes, and most of the time, it leads to marriage, with fewer divorces. But in the West, people date, fall in love, live together, and then marry, yet there's a 60% divorce rate. Why is that?"

Bhagyaraj thought it was a good question and told them he would ponder over it that night and return the next morning with an answer. The following day, when he visited again, his teacher asked if he had found an answer, to which Bhagyaraj replied, "Yes."

Vijay was eager to hear Bhagyaraj's thoughts. Bhagyaraj began, "Vijay, do you watch sports?" Vijay nodded and said, "Yes, uncle. I watch tennis, soccer, and cricket." Bhagyaraj then asked, "Would you prefer watching a match live or as a replay?" Vijay immediately answered, "Live, of course."

Bhagyaraj smiled and said, "The answer to your question is in the response you just gave." He continued, "In India, marriages are like watching a match 'live,' while in the West, they are like watching an 'action replay.'"

'In India, when a prospective bride and groom meet, with their families present, about 90% of the marriage is already decided. Both the boy and the girl trust that their parents have done their homework and found the best match for them. After this meeting, the wedding date is set. When the couple meets on their wedding night, it's often awkward and shy, but over time, they grow to love each other. Soon, children are born, and the couple's focus shifts to raising a family. They may realise they aren't an ideal couple, but they also understand that life isn't ideal, and expecting a perfect partner is unrealistic.'

"In the West, however, it's different. Marriage is usually not arranged, and families are less involved. Dating, love, living together, and sometimes getting pregnant before marriage are common. This doesn't mean one approach is right or wrong, but statistics show that over 60% of marriages in the West end in divorce."

"So, Vijay, that's my answer to your question," Bhagyaraj concluded with a knowing smile.

187. Bathroom Battles

About 50 years ago, my cousin lived with his parents and brother in a small one-bedroom apartment. He had a deep love for reading, especially comic books, and was rarely seen without one. He took his books everywhere—school, the living room, the bedroom, even to the dining table while eating. On many occasions, he even carried them into the bathroom.

One morning, his father was rushing to get to work. After shaving, he needed to take a shower but found the bathroom occupied. He waited for a bit, then called out, "What are you doing in there?"

His son replied, "I'm taking a bath."

After a few more minutes, his father, growing impatient, shouted, "If you're not out in one minute, I'm coming in!"

My cousin calmly responded, "If you barge in like that, then I won't take my bath!"

188. Chilling Expectations

In 1991, I was running a new business and had set up an office. The office was on the first floor, with an open terrace above it. Money was tight, and I couldn't afford a brand-new air conditioner, which cost around Rs 25,000 at the time. I had only Rs 5,000, so I bought a second- (or maybe third- or fourth-) hand air conditioner.

This poor old machine struggled to cool the room, barely managing to lower the temperature by 3 degrees Celsius. There was no false ceiling either, and with the summer heat outside reaching 37 degrees in the afternoons, the office felt like an oven. One day, a client wanted to visit. He insisted on meeting in my office, despite my attempts to dissuade him from coming during the scorching afternoon. I called it my "office," but it was more like a hot den.

To prepare for his visit, I turned on the air conditioner at 9 a.m., hoping it would make the room bearable by 2 p.m. I kept the room tightly shut, making sure no one entered, fearing that the heat would get inside.

At 2 p.m., the client arrived, and I nervously ushered him into the "air-conditioned" room. To my relief, he seemed comfortable, and I finally breathed easily. But then, he said something I will never forget: "Could you please turn on the air conditioner? It's really hot in here!"

189. Our Conscience

There are many differences between a human being and an animal. There are some commonalities also. The commonality between a human being and an animal is that both have the following equipment: the eyes, the ears, the skin, the nose, and the tongue. It is through these that seeing, hearing, feeling (through the skin), smelling, and tasting are possible. The process of evolution took off from the mineral age to the plant age, to the animal age, to the human age.

The humans are different from the animals in that they have the equipment called "Intellect" to discriminate/discern. They know the difference between right and wrong; they are supposed to have morals, ethics, and values. Morals and values are generally personal, and ethics are generally professional/social.

One of the morals/values a human being is presumed to have is a clear "Conscience." Conscience is that part of the mind that discerns between right and wrong. It is more than just a "gut instinct;" our conscience is a moral muscle. A story to exemplify:

There lived a man who was a thief. That was his profession. He was good at it. He lived with his wife and son in a house. Just like many parents who want their children to do the same profession as theirs when they grew up, this thief also wanted his son to become a thief. Not just a thief but a "master thief." He wanted to leave a rich legacy behind!

The thief had taken his son, who worked as an apprentice, to many places where they stole and escaped without anyone getting noticed. He was so good at that. When the thief thought that his son now had all the exposure to thievery, he wanted his son to graduate and prove that he had earned the worthiness of being a good thief – just like him.

One day the thief told his son, "You now have all the expertise to break open a house, steal and get away with the booty without getting noticed and getting caught; I want you to prove yourself that you can handle the job independently. This is to prove your mettle. Tonight, you will go to this address, break open the lock silently, get inside, steal the valuables and get back as silently as you had got in. Make no mistake, you will decamp with the valuables and return in about 2 hours. Leave by 11 pm. I will be expecting you by 1 am."

The son was going to steal for the first time independently. He was anxious. He was worried. Taking a deep breath, he bid goodbye to his parents and walked towards the prescribed address. His father had taught him the art, and the son meticulously opened the lock, went to the right place where people normally keep their valuables, and embarked on his return journey with the booty.

It was 1 am, and the father was sitting on a chair outside the house waiting for his son to arrive. Time slowly became 2 am, then 3 am, then 4, then 5. The father got very restless. He thought maybe his son had got caught and been handed over to the police or got thrashed by the owner. He was now profusely sweating and feverishly pacing up and down on the road in front of his house. Around 6 am, the son appeared, and the father first saw his son's hand. It was empty. He was aghast. He saw his son's face; it looked crestfallen.

The father was truly worried and walked towards his son and asked him, "What happened? Is everything alright?" The son's face looked forlorn and he cried. "Sorry dad, I failed you," he told his dad. "What happened? Were you caught or were you not able to break in?" "No, dad," replied his son. "I broke in easily, quickly found the location of the valuables, got them, put them in the bag that you had given me, closed the door behind me and silently started walking back." Saying this, he sobbed and said, "I failed you, dad, I failed you."

Tell me what happened," the adoring father told his son. The son said, "Soon after I left the address with the booty, I had a strange feeling that someone was watching me." "So, who was watching you?" asked the father. The son replied, "Everyone was watching me; the moon was watching me, the trees were watching me, beyond all this my conscience was watching me." "Only the house owner and his family did not watch me." "I have failed, dad; I have failed you." As often as we hear something like, "Operation success, but patient died!"

The dad prompted his son to proceed telling as to what he did with the valuables. The son said, "As much as it was easy to break the lock, find the valuables, undoing was not that difficult. I kept back the valuables in the same place, closed the door behind, on the way home sat under a tree and contemplated about my future."

Sorry, Dad. I will not pursue this profession. I am not comfortable with what I did. I will go and do some other work that is not against my morals and values. I also request you to consider another profession, making your dad feel bewildered.

We might think that no one is watching our actions. In fact, everything is watched by the "Silent Witness," which is our soul or consciousness, and our soul is connected to everything in the universe. Whatever we do, we are being watched. Let our actions be noble; Existence will take care of the rest. You become what you think all day long...

This is how "Karma" works. The Law of Causation: Cause-and-Effect. As you sow, so you reap.

Conscience is the voice of God in the soul....

"Watch your thoughts; they become words."

"Watch your words; they become actions."

"Watch your actions; they become habits."

"Watch your habits; they become your character."

"Watch your character; it becomes your destiny."--- Lao Tzu

Never do anything against conscience even if the state demands it – Albert Einstein

190. Gods in Everyday Life

Writer Sujatha had narrated this incident:

I had just started a new job, and after work, I would wait for the bus near the Bangalore Corporation gate. There were Tempo Traveler cabs that picked up passengers heading towards Electronic City for five rupees. But on the last day of the month, I had no cash left, so I would often walk home, thinking the day wasn't too hot.

One day, I found myself standing there for a long time, uncertain about how I'd get home. I decided to get down at Bommanahalli, borrow some money from the bookseller, and catch a Tempo Traveler. All through the ride, I was anxious — would the bookshop be open, and would the seller lend me five rupees? I worried too that the driver might be angry if I delayed the journey.

When all the other passengers had disembarked, I approached the driver and said, "Brother, please excuse me, I'll go to the shop and get the money." The driver looked at me calmly and replied, "No problem, brother. Just close the door properly and go." In his eyes, I saw a gentle sympathy, understanding my plight without a word.

That experience gave me a sense of resilience. People everywhere, without hesitation, can understand the struggles of others. This unseen compassion, I thought, is what makes the world go round — it's what people call God.

Nearly 10 years later, I had bought a modern car and commuted on the same road to the office every day. Each time I thought of that Tempo Traveler driver. In his memory, I started picking up old men waiting at bus stops, asking them where they were headed, and dropping them off. It felt like a small way to repay the kindness that had been shown to me.

One day, while walking back from work near Kendriya Sadan, I heard someone call "Sir" from behind. An elderly woman with frail bones approached me, holding out a prescription from St. John's Hospital. She had a few pills, a bottle of Protinex, and a medical slip. I didn't know why she chose me to ask for help, but I immediately reached for a 200-rupee note in my pocket. Before I could give it to her, she softly said, "I don't need money, brother. I can't walk properly, but if you could buy me the medicine, I'd be grateful."

Even in her poverty and old age, she carried herself with dignity. Her words reminded me of my own hesitation and embarrassment from 20 years ago when I had asked that driver for help. It was as though that moment had come full circle.

I gently sat her down and told her, "Wait here, Mom. I'll get the medicine." After wandering around, I found a small pharmacy open. Two young Marwari men were arranging medicines. I handed them the prescription and asked, "How much will it cost?" They looked at it and said, "This will be 776 rupees, but only one of the medicines is available from another company. Is that alright?"

I didn't know and told them, "It's for an elderly woman I don't know. She asked me to buy it for her." The pharmacist glanced at me for a moment and quietly started typing on the computer. After a while, he handed me the medicine and two receipts, smiling as he returned some money.

I was moved by his quiet trust in my words. Even though I was the one directly asked for help, this young man, who had no connection to the situation, believed in my story and felt the same compassion. Isn't the person who helps just on faith greater than those of us who are directly asked for help?

I returned to the old woman, handed her the medicine, and slipped the 200-rupee note into her hands. As I walked away, I reflected on how, despite the 20 years that had passed, the kindness of people hadn't changed.

Some scientists say the earth's inner core may be rotating in the opposite direction now, but I believe that the axis of compassion and mercy among humans still spins the same way. The kindness that the driver showed me, and the generosity of the Marwari youth — these moments, I realised, are what people call God. God is that unexpected mercy that flows from one person to another.

191. The Attitude in Good Relationships

Attitude is the way a person thinks, feels, acts, and behaves and largely depends on the person's value system. It could be right or wrong. Again, right or wrong depends on who is seeing it!

An analogy to explain the attitude in good relationships. Consider the two winged small social insects – the common fly and the honeybee. There is a powerful lesson one could learn from this.

Both the honeybee and the common fly are 4-winged insects, but their perspectives are different. The honeybee works all year round and saves food for the rainy day. They leave their hives when the weather gets warmer in search of flowers, and flowers bloom during summer. Once they find a flower, they use their long tongue to suck the nectar and store it in their second stomach. The second stomach is also called a honey stomach.

The honey bee reaches the hive and passes the nectar into the mouth of another bee after chewing it for 30 minutes. The second, the third, and so the nectar from flowers become honey, which is stored in honeycomb, which acts as jars and is made out of wax. The bees flap their wings over the honeycomb to make the honey thicker and not watery, and once this is done, the bees seal the honeycomb with the honey by wax for usage later.

The mindset of a honeybee is to gather nectar from flowers and make honey. The honeybee travels a long way just in search of flowers. It may travel through miles and miles of garbage, filth, and excrement, its focus is only on the flowers. It doesn't get distracted by any amount of garbage and filth. It visits every flower, small or big, doesn't damage the flower but helps pollination in flowers inadvertently!

Every life organism is tuned to perform a certain activity. Nature never repeats. Insects are attuned to their instincts. Take, for example, a common fly. The common fly is wired differently and totally different from a honeybee. For instance, when the fly travels over a rose garden or any garden with an enormous number of flowers, it doesn't get attracted to it. Its perspective is different. It gets attracted to filth, garbage, excrement, slush, and uncleanness. If one watches closely, a fly doesn't get attracted to a healthy human body; but if the body has wounds, cuts, bruises, the fly gets attracted to it and forages into it. The mindset of a fly is the opposite of that of a honeybee, to forage into filth and rubbish.

The honeybee teaches us a valuable lesson. It focuses on the essence, that is nectar. It doesn't get distracted by anything else. It teaches us a valuable lesson to improve our relationships and the quality of life. It teaches us the art of focusing on the positives and dealing suitably with the faults in each other. There will be faults in every person, everywhere. There is no shortage of things to complain about. We should be like the honeybee which concentrates only on the nectar, the essence. We should likewise focus on the goodness in each one of us and obliterate their faults. No one is perfect in all counts and no one is imperfect in all measures.

It requires no effort to see the flaws in others. Fault finding is an abominable habit. The more we give in to it, the more we become obsessed by it. In relationships, it is important to have honest, well-wishing communication, focusing on the positives and dealing graciously with the negatives in a constructive manner. We should learn to bring out the positives when we deal with people. By doing so, we ourselves would be bringing out the best qualities from within ourselves to reach a higher form of ourselves.

To be like a honeybee or like a fly... The choice is ours...

192. Nature's Behaviour is Nothing but a Reflection of Our Own Mental Attitude

The world operates on a Cause-and-Effect principle, simply termed as the Laws of Causation. They are:

1. An effect cannot be without a cause.

2. Effects are the cause itself in a different form.

3. From the Effect if the Cause is removed, nothing remains.

If one could live in complete awareness of these laws, further learning can be stopped!

Man's technological advancement has done enormous good to mankind. Distances have shrunk by the invention of airplanes, automobiles, communication across time zones at any instant, the latest medicines to cure from common cold to cancer, modern equipment in farming to improve efficiency, the world of computers, and many breakthroughs in science and technology thereby improving the standard of living and life expectancy. However, in this competitive world, the quality of life has deteriorated. Desires to possess the many things available in this world have increased, not because I need them but because of family, social, and status pressures.

There are a lot of forces which we think we could control, but there are a zillion forces that we don't know of, also acting based on the Law of Causation. It is a Universal law that when our behaviour is perfect, nature shall also behave perfectly. The recent El Nino, the climate change due to deforestation, soil erosion, constructing towns and villages on lakes and water bodies, heat trapped at the surface of the earth because of Greenhouse gases, thereby making the earth hotter and so on... are testimonies of the aftermath of the actions of man's ego and selfish desires.

Man alone disobeys laws, and he alone suffers in this world. There is no suffering for the plants, animals, or the birds. They all implicitly obey the laws of instincts and impulses. Man alone does not obey; he asks, "Why should I obey the law?" And as a result, he creates all the sorrows in the world. The human signature is there in all the sorrows of this world. The sorrows are all man-made. The disharmony is created because of our ego and selfish desires.

Mighty phenomenal forces are called Devas. Deva does not mean God. Deva means the mighty phenomenal forces – Varuna, the waters, Vayu, the air, Agni, the fire, Indra, the mighty power of the rain. Each is a phenomenal force. This has been given such names in those days as God. The Devas are phenomenal forces on which the puny human beings have no control.

When the people in the world cherish the other people in the world with the spirit of Cooperation and Coordination, when you change the style of life, sinking your differences and together come and work in the world outside, that the Deva or the mighty phenomenal forces shall cherish you back. This is a Universal law told in the Scriptures. When our behaviour is perfect, nature shall behave perfectly. When we are crazy mad, nature, which is nothing but our behaviour's true reflection, also gets crazy mad!

We complain that nature is so erratic. It has been hotter in summer, very cold in winter, rains during odd seasons, inundation of coastal areas and the like, not knowing that we ourselves are the cause for this predicament! If we change, the actions of the

Phenomenal Forces would also change. Nature reflects man and his behaviour. We should invoke nature by living a beautiful life – with love and kindness, with tolerance, compassion, mercy for others, and live harmoniously.

Nature will change its mood in reciprocation to our mental attitude. When we become a healthy person, our reflection in the mirror shows a healthy person. Nature's behaviour is a mental reflection of our mental attitude in life.

193. Work-life Balance

I was a cricketer during my younger days. I was very good playing in the nets, but when it came to "live matches," I did not live up to the promise and expectations of many! So much so, when the souvenir of our "Grand Prix cricket club" came, introducing the cricketers, Mr S. Ravindran (then CEO, Sundaram Health Foundation) wrote this about me: "S.Ramkumar - Steals the heart of everybody with his dazzling display of batting and bowling (but only in the nets)!" Our club was in the First Division of TNCA and became the gateway for aspiring cricketers who got employment through cricket in banks, Port Trust, Corporates... and there were the likes of L.Sivaramakrishnan and W.V. Raman who stood out in their class and went on to play for India. They put in many hours into cricket.

They played for India because of their talent and sheer hard work. I knew that I was not meant to be a professional cricketer since I was not talented in cricket but was prepared to work hard in some other field of my interest!

While my friends were focusing on playing high-level cricket, I was a cheerleader and well-wisher of our club. This was after my engineering and three years of work in Mumbai and Vizag in MNCs. I wanted to make it big in life. I did not know how?!!

That was the time when Vadyar Boats, an FRP lifeboat manufacturing company, gave me a breakthrough. They gave me Rs 250 to check the insulation resistance of all electrical loads and give a report. I gladly took it. I suddenly realised that I had become an entrepreneur! The next job I got was erecting sodium vapour lamps, the next was consultancy work in instrumentation for their first-ever enclosed lifeboat in India (the first one ever in India for ships used in oil-carrying tankers), besides maintenance of Bata showrooms, electrical work for installation of PCs' mainframes, then site preparation for mainframes, interior designing, turnkey projects, and the list was endless. Our company would have installed more computers than anyone else pan India at that time. This was the time when LS and WV also played for India! Hard work pays!

Thank you, LS, WV!!

Riding one hundred kilometres by bike every day, in the beginning of my career, foregoing lunch on several occasions, sixteen hours working per day, doing many contracts in Chennai, Bangalore, Mumbai, all during the first 10 years since the age of twenty-six. There was no question of work-life balance. It was work, work most of the time. When someone wants to make it big, there have to be a few big compromises. Especially as an aspiring entrepreneur with high goals or a young high-performance manager working for large companies - You can't catch two rabbits at the same time!"

In the initial stages of one's professional career, one needs to focus on work, slog it out to meet professional and business goals... invariably at the end of it, you would find the magical work-life balance. Trying to find both earlier in life, according to me, you would lose out in both – work and life. You have to give up something in order to get something bigger. A rocket uses more than 90% of its fuel during take-off and the remaining fuel for the rest of its journey!! Anything well begun is half done.

You can't reach the top of the corporate ladder working for 40 hours a week. You can't expect to be promoted if you leave the office by 5 pm. You can't reduce your weight if you have your eyes constantly on kesar-pista! You have to work for many hours at work. Not just hard work but more work within less time. You have to be the first one to reach the office and the last to leave the office. Work gives meaning to life. As you start getting successful, all your other plans in life would set in. Work-Life balance would happen subsequently and would rest on pillars of hard work and commitment.

Once after a certain age, work-life balance would become an important factor to determine the balance between the two. Maintaining work-life balance helps reduce stress and helps prevent burnout in the workplace.

The quality time you spend with your family is directly proportional to the quality time you give at work. What you do after 8 pm during family time determines how you do at 9 am during office time! By creating a work environment that prioritises work-life balance, employers can save money and maintain a healthier workforce.

Many people feel that employers aren't responsible for employees' work-life balance; the fact of the matter would be that employers may encounter a higher rate of turnover, absenteeism, and lower productivity. Employers can help ensure proper work-home balance among their employees, and this would result in

1. Increase in Engagement levels at work

2. Lesser burnouts

3. More Mindfulness resulting in creativity, productivity

This can be done by:

Encouraging time off by telling them to go on short vacations.

1. Flexi hours of working

2. Providing laptop and working from home

To be able to maintain a healthy work-life balance, the most important things that people can do are:

1. Exercise. Exercise increases happy hormones endorphins. It reduces stress.

2. Meditation reduces the number of thoughts. From Beta state you can shift your consciousness to Alpha state.

3. Limit time wasting activities and people. Spend quality time with family with the mobile in silent mode.

4. Implement short breaks throughout the day to loosen out.

5. See comedy pictures.

6. Take it easy. Life is a tragedy for those who feel, it's a comedy for those who think!!

194. The Power of Patience

Patience is a Virtue. Patience is a person's ability to wait for something without getting irritated. The ability to wait for something without being angry or upset is a valuable quality in a person. In today's world, instant results to experience pleasure or fulfilment have become the order of the day.

Twenty-twenty cricket is an example... A test match needs more attention, tenacity, energy, focus, cool and calm mind, determination and really tests the cricketer over five days, whereas T20 is a power game. One over could alter the course of the match! But people love T20 because you can see power and results in three and a half hours over popcorn and coke! Just like a film!

The advantages of being patient are it allows you time for strategic thinking and completely evaluating a situation. Things have to fall in place and it takes time. A flight is delayed, you need to wait. There is no point in jumping up and down for jumping up and down does not bring the flight earlier!! Board exams have got postponed. So, what do we do? "WAIT." The flight will come; the exams will happen. If we can keep our patience and wait for our turn to come, we will definitely get what we want. "WAITING" or "Being Patient" is a mature way of handling life and is a spiritual quality.

Once Chatrapathi Shivaji, the great king from India, lost his way going from one fort to the other. He looked from a hilltop and could see a hut at a distance with a dim light coming out of it. Night was approaching fast, and he quickly made his way to the hut. An old woman, upon seeing Shivaji, thought that the soldier belonged to Chatrapathi Shivaji's army, welcomed him, gave water to wash himself, and after a little rest gave him piping hot food. Upon seeing the food, which he had not eaten for long, he dug his hand deep into the rice and curry and took a handful into his mouth!! The hot food burned his fingers, and he almost immediately brought his hand down from his mouth, spilling a lot of food.

The old woman nodded her head and said, "Young soldier, you seem to be in a great bit of impatience and haste, like your master, Chatrapathi Shivaji; that's why you have burned your fingers and spilled the food also." Shivaji was astonished at the remark and asked the woman why she thought that his master Shivaji was always acting in haste and being impatient. The woman replied, "Shivaji, instead of fighting and capturing smaller forts, he is hell-bent on attempting the larger forts. He is just like you wanting to take a large chunk of meal from the centre; instead, if you had started taking your meal from the corners which would have been relatively cooler, you wouldn't have burned your fingers." She continued, "Shivaji should have captured the smaller forts, strengthened his position, and then attempted to conquer the bigger forts – this way the loss of soldiers would be minimal," much to the astonishment of Shivaji. He diligently carried out as per what the old woman said. "Haste makes waste," he pondered!

We prefer to change our decisions than to have patience. It usually bothers us to postpone our desires. When we think that we have to wait, our mind is perturbed and it does something to us to get up and act! Instead of controlling the mind, the mind starts controlling us!

Buddha and his disciples went on a long journey crossing several cities and territories. They saw a lake at a distance. Buddha told the most impatient of his disciples to go fetch water for all of them to drink. The disciple went to fetch water; a wagon of oxen crossed the lake and made it dirty. The disciple turned back and went to Buddha and told him that the water is muddy and so did not bring it. Buddha told him after half an hour to go back and fetch water. The disciple went and came back and said the same thing, "It's still muddy."

Again, after a while, Buddha told him to fetch water. Irritatingly, the disciple went and saw crystal clear water. He filled up and gave it to Buddha and others. The Buddha looked at the disciple and explained, "You waited and let it be!" Therefore, the mud settled down on its own and it has now become clear. Your mind is also like that. When it is muddy, you will have to let it be. On the contrary, if you are patient, it will reach balance on its own accord. Everything will pass on its own if you choose not to hold on to it. Patience is the Lord's call for our character to not merely engage in passive endurance but active perseverance.

The farmer sows the seed and "waits" - for nature to take over. He has done what he was supposed to do to the best of his ability. He "doesn't wait for," instead he just waits. "Waiting for" will give sleepless nights; the best thing is to just WAIT.

I have heard of pregnant ladies recording their weight every day. It seems the fetus grows at about 25 grams per day. In case the weight increase is not as per their calculations, they get impatient and worried!

Patience is one of the key parameters in the materialistic journey and spiritual journey as well. It is a key to achieving your goals. It's better that the decisions taken by you are carefully considered, since everything needs time. Good things take time. Have patience.

www.ingramcontent.com/pod-product-compliance
Lightning Source LLC
Chambersburg PA
CBHW032004150726
47990CB00005B/1836

9798895569603